I LOVE
THIS GAME!

KIRBY PUCKETT

I LOVE THIS GAME!

●MY LIFE AND BASEBALL●

HarperCollinsPublishers

Photographs follow page 148.

HarperCollins books may be purchased for educational, business, or sales promotional use. For information, please write: Special Markets Department, Harper-Collins Publishers, Inc., 10 East 53rd Street, New York, NY 10022.

FIRST EDITION

Designed by Claudyne Bianco

Library of Congress Cataloging-in-Publication Data

Puckett, Kirby.
    I love this game! : my life and baseball / Kirby Puckett.—1st ed.
       p.   cm.
    ISBN 0-06-017710-1
    1. Puckett, Kirby. 2. Baseball players—United States—Biography. I. Title.
GV865.P83A3   1993
796.357'092—dc20   92-53343
[B]

93 94 95 96 97 ❖/HC 10 9 8 7 6 5 4 3 2 1

IN MEMORY OF MOM AND DAD;
AND FOR YOU, TONYA,
AND CATHERINE AND KIRBY JR.,
AND ALL MY FAMILY AND FRIENDS.

ACKNOWLEDGMENTS

First of all, thanks to the friends, family members, baseball personnel, and baseball players who contributed to this story: Rob Antony, George Brophy, Ellsworth Brown, Tom Brunansky, Randy Bush, Mark Davidson, Carmen Dugger, Cal Ermer, Alvaro Espinosa, Billy Gardner, Dan Gladden, Brian Harper, Delores Henderson, Margaret Hudson, Lance Johnson, Dewey Kalmer, Tom Kelly, Rimzi Kiratli, Chuck Knoblauch, Shane Mack, Charlie Manuel, James McGhee, Andy MacPhail, Ray Miller, Al Newman (a special thanks here), Tony Oliva, Jim Rantz, Harold Reynolds, Laura Singleton, June Sinkfield, Rick Stelmaszek, Art Stewart, Bob Symonds, Lin Terwilliger, Wayne Terwilliger, Frank Viola, Ron Washington, and Jim Wiesner.

I also thank Steve Rausch and Wendie Erickson from the Twins' Media Relations office; Bob Jansen, librarian for the Minneapolis *Star Tribune;* Marcy Winkelman with the Children's Heart Fund in Minnesota; researchers Nicole Bryan and Scott Eberly; Steve Gaskins and Cathy Larsen; Patty and Mike Bryan and Joe Spieler.

I thank my editor at HarperCollins, Wendy Wolf, even

though she's a Yankee fan, for her enthusiastic work on this book; her assistant, Eileen Campion; and Mike Leonard of the HarperCollins sales team, the man who really wanted this book published and a Minnesota Twins fanatic.

This book, like many other activities in my life, would not be possible without the help of my agent, Ron Shapiro, and his associate, Michael Maas; and their wonderful support crew. Thanks for everything.

Finally, I thank my wife, Tonya, for the time and attention and support she devoted to this book from beginning to end.

I LOVE
THIS GAME!

ONE

Who knows, but I might owe my baseball career and my two World Series rings to the hiring policies of the Ford Motor Company. If Ford hadn't laid me off in 1979 I might be working on its assembly line right now. I was eighteen and had just graduated from high school in Chicago, and I thought I was a good enough ballplayer to play in the minors, maybe even in the majors. A few other people thought so, too, and my mom said there was *no doubt* in her mind that I would be a big league ballplayer. But moms are always that way.

I wasn't thinking about a career in automotives, but I wasn't really focused on pro ball, either. I knew I was tired of going to school and that the best college scholarship offer I had was from a school in Miami—a good junior college program, but too far from home. As the ninth and last of the Puckett kids, I was Mom and Dad's baby. That's the truth. I wanted to stay close to them. So I told my parents, hey, I'm eighteen, I'm a man, or almost a man, I don't want to go to school right now, I want to take a year to see what the real world is like.

That's how I came to work at the Ford plant on Torrence Avenue, on the south side of Chicago. I got the job with the help of a friend who already worked there. You talk about fast work!

The guy across the line and I were in charge of laying the carpet in Thunderbirds. If you own one of those vintage models, I might have installed the rug in that beauty. The pieces of carpet were stacked up beside me, already arranged in the right order to match the color of the Thunderbirds coming down the line. I didn't have to think about what color went in what car—which was good, because I didn't have time to think! We had less than a minute to throw a rug in each car and fit it over some bolts sticking out of the floor. The next station down the line would then put in the seats and bolt everything down. I liked the work. I don't know what it would be like to toil on the line for thirty years, but it was a great job for a kid just out of high school.

I rode the bus back and forth to the plant—an express bus, and if I missed it, I was screwed. Tough to get to Torrence Avenue otherwise. So I didn't miss it. I made eight or nine dollars an hour at Ford and some overtime, too, and that was a fortune. I brought home $500 every week after taxes, but I still had to convince Mom and Dad to accept a little of my pay to help with the household expenses.

But at Ford then—I don't know what the policy is now— you could work at that plant for ninety days before you became an official unionized employee, and they let me go on the eighty-ninth day. I know they didn't fire me because I wasn't doing the job. I *was* doing the job! I just reached that ninety-day limit, I'm sure.

I could not have dreamed that one afternoon less than five years after I walked out of that Ford factory for the last time, I would walk into center field at Anaheim Stadium in California as a major league ballplayer for the Minnesota Twins, and on my way to owning those two championship rings. A few guys are headed for the majors right from the sixth grade, it seems. Chuck Knoblauch, the Twins' young second baseman, was that way, apparently. Barry Bonds, Cal Ripken, Jr., Ken Griffey, Jr.—they were all *targeted* for the majors. They knew it, the coaches knew it, the scouts knew it, the general managers knew it. But the rest of us need breaks. The world is full of .400 hitters in high school and .350 hitters in college—many of them helped along by the aluminum bats. Something has to get you noticed and make you stand out. And the timing has to be right and you need some luck—or at least I did. And the first of the series of good breaks that brought me to Anaheim Stadium was losing that job at Ford.

When the *final* break came, I couldn't believe what was happening. I was playing with the Toledo Mud Hens, the Twins' Triple-A team, and the 1984 season was only a few weeks old. Our hotel in Old Orchard Beach, Maine, right outside Portland, looked like an Army barracks and was right next to the railroad tracks. Those trains sounded like they were coming straight through the rooms. The whole building shook. Our manager, Cal Ermer, joked that a derailment would have killed all of us and really messed up the Twins' farm system.

It had rained for three straight days and it was raining again that evening. My roomie, Tack Wilson, and I were watching TV. It was about seven o'clock and we were bored. We'd been watching TV and playing cards and going out to eat and coming back to watch more TV for three straight days. Boring. Nothing to do.

Our rooms didn't have telephones, so the hotel clerk had to walk over in the rain to tell Cal Ermer that he had a phone call from Calvin Griffith, the owner of the Twins at that time. Then Cal had to walk over to our room. He knocked on the door. Tack let him in.

He looked at me. "Congratulations, kid. You're going to the big show."

"The big show": They really do say that in the minors. I jumped up. "Who, me?!"

"No, me. Yeah, *you*. Congratulations. They want you in Anaheim tomorrow afternoon. Got a flight for you in the morning already."

The first thing I did was get on the phone with my mother. My dad had passed away several years before. You know Mom was excited. She called all my brothers and sisters, and they all got excited. Maybe they got some sleep that night. I didn't. All I could think about were the players on the Twins—Kent Hrbek, Gary Gaetti, Frank Viola—and on the Angels, stars I'd never met like Reggie Jackson, Bobby Grich, Dick Schofield, Doug DeCinces, *Reggie Jackson*. I was scared to death. But I also believed I could do the job. They always tell you in baseball, at every level, that if you didn't belong, you wouldn't be here. I was a pretty confident baseball player—always had been—and I believed it. Plus Cal Ermer told me that rainy night in Maine that I'd find it *easier* playing in the big leagues. The lights are better for hitting, Cal said, the pitchers have better control and keep the ball around the plate more often, the fields are better, the meal money is better, everything is better. He was sure right about the lights. I never played with decent lighting in a night game until I went to the majors. At most of the fields the Mud Hens visited, the lights didn't really do anything until the seventh inning, when it was good and dark.

I found out later that the final decision to call me up to

the majors had been made in a hotel in Seattle, where the Twins were playing before they went down the coast to Anaheim. Calvin Griffith; Billy Gardner, the manager at that time; Tom Kelly, the third base coach; Rick Stelmaszek, long-time Twins coach; and some other guys had gotten together in Calvin's suite to deal with their problem in center field. Jim Eisenreich, the regular outfielder, was sidelined with an illness and no one knew when or if he could play again. (It turned out to be Tourette's syndrome, and Jim never played again for the Twins. But he did play for the Kansas City Royals.) And I guess no one was very happy with the performance—especially on defense—of Darrell Brown, the backup center fielder on the team.

Kelly and Stelmaszek went out on a limb for me. Some of the people in the organization wanted to keep me down in Triple-A with the Mud Hens a little longer. When the idea of bringing me up from Toledo had first come up a few weeks earlier, Cal Ermer thought I might not be ready. I only had two years in the minors and I had skipped Double-A ball entirely, and probably could have used a little more *seasoning*, as they say. Plus, for the first time in my minor league career, I was not hitting the ball well. The hits weren't falling. If I got off to a bad start in the majors my confidence might be ruined forever; a few more months with less pressure might make all the difference. And somebody even produced some statistics showing that my "chances per game" playing center field so far in '84 were way below average for Triple-A. That statistic supposedly shows what kind of jump the fielder gets on the ball and how fast he is.

But Kelly and Stelmaszek must have said, "Forget those stats, we *know* Puckett can go get the ball in the field. Can he hit major league pitching? We're not sure, but he can field."

They were sure about my fielding because they knew me a lot better than anyone else in that hotel room. They'd worked with me during two Instructional Leagues in the fall in Florida. After some discussion, they convinced Calvin Griffith and Billy Gardner to take the chance. I wasn't worried about my .263 average with the Mud Hens; we'd only played twenty-one games and I was hitting the ball hard, if not always *accurately*. But the owner and the big league manager could have said, Let's wait. And then who knows what might have happened.

May 7, 1984. I fly out of Portland about six in the morning and am scheduled to arrive in Anaheim at four that afternoon. No problem—until I get to Atlanta and find out that the plane there has a crack in the windshield or the defroster isn't working or something. I'm sitting around waiting, looking at my watch, worrying. Really worrying. I've got $10 in my pocket. After a few hours and no plane yet, I'm *panicking* and don't have any phone number to call. All Cal Ermer told me was that someone would meet me at the airport at Anaheim at four o'clock.

I finally arrived in California at six P.M. and looked around for somebody looking for me. Nobody there. Panicking again. Then I decided that the people in the airport would know what to do about this stranded baseball player.

"Excuse me, do you know if there's anybody here to pick up Kirby Puckett with the Minnesota Twins?"

I've got my bags in my hands. The guy said, "Sorry, I don't know anything about it."

Finally I settled down and asked myself what a normal person would do in this situation. Get in a cab. But I didn't have any money. I also knew that the cab drivers in Chicago usually don't trust you in that kind of situation, so I didn't think they would in Los Angeles. But the cabbie I got was a nice guy from Japan—as he told me during the ride. I told him that I was a minor league ballplayer just called up to the major leagues, and that I only had $10 with me so he'd have to wait at the stadium while I went inside to get my meal money to pay him. No problem, he said. But when we got there the meter read about $60! This story has been recounted many times within the Twins organization, and that number changes. I say $60. I still doubted that the driver really trusted me, so I left one bag with him and took the other bag and told the man at the door that I was Kirby Puckett, just called up to the big leagues by the Twins.

"Oh yeah, yeah. Kirby Puckett. Come on in." That impressed me immediately. In one day I'd gone from "Who are you?" to "Oh, yeah, no problem, come on in!"

I ran into the stadium, asked where the visiting clubhouse was, and finally found it. Mike Robertson, the traveling secretary for the Twins at the time, met me and I told him I had a cab waiting outside and needed my meal money to pay the guy. Mike laughed and explained that the team would pay for the cab ride. He gave me a hundred-dollar bill and I ran out and gave it to the cab driver and told him, "Hey, you take $85." I shook his hand and wanted to kiss him. You don't find trusting people like that often. I wish I had taken his name. Free tickets anytime for that cab driver.

When I got back to the clubhouse with all my bags one of the coaches came over and said, "Hey, Kirby Puckett, nice to meet you. Billy Gardner wants you to take some BP right now. Hurry up and get dressed." So I threw on the uniform they gave me, checked out my new number, 34, and walked up the ramp to the dugout and the field. When I stepped onto the field I saw more people in the stands for batting practice than came to a lot of the Mud Hen games. I was going from a stadium with eight or nine thousand seats to one with fifty, sixty, seventy thousand. You're talking *totally* different ballpark. You can ask any ballplayer and he'll tell you about that first view of the stands as a major leaguer. It's a thrill. But me—I was frantic again.

Richard Yett, a Twins prospect doing rehab work, I think, was throwing batting practice. I stepped in, hit the ball pretty solidly, nothing spectacular, and then ran around the bases. Billy Gardner came over and introduced himself as the manager of the club and said I looked tired, a little jet-lagged.

"Not really, coach, I'm ready to go. I'm a little tired but I'm ready."

"No. I'll tell you what. I want you to sit on the bench tonight, eat some sunflower seeds, chew some gum, relax and watch the guys play. But tomorrow night you'll be my starting center fielder."

Apparently I had been written into the lineup, but then my name was erased when I showed up so late. I now know from experience that the veterans on the team are always anxious to get a look at any rookie, especially one most of them have never met. Randy Bush says today, almost nine years later, that the players couldn't believe what they saw: this short, squat guy, definitely not your classic major league build. Not even a minor league build: I was a mere five-foot-eight, 175 pounds (that's all, back then). I know for a fact that some of the Twins took one look at me and thought the organization was making a big mistake if they thought I was the center fielder of the future for the Minnesota Twins.

I went around and introduced myself, and some guys

came over to me. Bush loves to tell the story about how he came over but before he could say a word I grabbed his hand and blurted out, "Hello, Mr. Bush, it's a pleasure to meet you. I've been a big fan for years!" He roars about that because he'd been in the big leagues less than two years himself, and was not exactly a headliner.

Bush swears I called everyone in the clubhouse *mister*, all humble and polite. Maybe I did. I'd never met a lot of these guys. They were all big and confident and veterans, practically. Sure I called them mister. Hrbek also had the number I had wanted, 14, Ernie Banks's number. But was I going to ask this guy to switch and give me his number?! My second choice was 24, Willie Mays's number. I looked around and saw Tom Brunansky wearing 24. I figured he could keep his number, too. Hey, I think I'll just keep this number, 34. It suits me fine.

I didn't play that night. I sat back and watched Darrell Brown play center field. After I'd settled in with the Twins, the guys gave me a hard time later about taking away Darrell's job. But you don't think that way as a ballplayer.

May 8, 1984. I would play my first big league game that night. Of course I called my mother in the morning to tell her I was starting that night, and she was all excited and saying, "I told you so. I'm proud of you. I said you were going to be a major leaguer." I was as happy for her as for myself.

Before batting practice I was sitting on the bench, looking around, nervous, when Reggie Jackson comes over. Some reporters are standing around, too. Reggie offers his hand and says, "Your name's Puckett, right?"

"Yes, Mr. Jackson." I'm pretty sure that time I did say mister. "Nice to meet you, Mr. Jackson."

"It looks like you hit them a long way."

"No, just a few singles."

Then Reggie goes, "Another singles hitter! What am I doing shaking your hand, then?"

Everyone got a big laugh out of that. I guess I laughed, too.

I wasn't laughing when I stepped into the box for my first big league at-bat. A regular-sized crowd—fifteen to twenty thousand—was in the stands. Jim Slaton was standing on the mound. I'm nervous, of course, but my first at-bat I hit a bullet between short and third. I don't remember the count, believe it or not—but chances are it was the first pitch, since I swing at so many of them! Dick Schofield backhands it and the throw barely beats me to the bag. A bang-bang play but I'm out. And I look back at Schofield and think, "*Man*, in Triple-A that's a hit. If this is how it's going to be in the big leagues, I'm in trouble. I'm in big trouble. I need those infield hits."

The second time up I'm still excited, adrenaline flowing, nervous but okay. I line a single up the middle but before I have a chance to celebrate, Tom Kelly, coaching at third base, flashes the steal sign. We'd gone over the signs that afternoon. I think, "Wow! I've made it now." I take off and steal second easy. Not even close. Before I know it John Castino, one of the slickest-fielding second basemen you ever saw, gets a base hit behind me and I score my first major league run. Guys are pounding me on the back in the dugout.

Next time up, Slaton still pitching, I get a single to right. So now I'm two-for-three. Next time, a hit to left. Three-for-four. Final time up, another hit up the middle. Four-for-five in my first major league game, good enough for the record books, somebody tells me: the ninth player to get four hits in his major league debut. And I caught everything they hit to me in center field, too, as Kelly and Stelmaszek had promised.

Billy Gardner mentioned to me later that year that my debut was the opposite of what happened to Willie Mays. I had been playing so-so in the minors before being called up, then started off gangbusters in the majors. Willie was hitting .400-plus in the minors, then went one-for-twenty-five his first week in the majors. I guess almost every struggling rookie is told the Willie Mays story, for inspiration. I'm just glad I didn't need it myself those first games.

Cal Ermer had predicted in the hotel room in Old Orchard Beach, Maine, that I'd get four hits my first major league game. I forgot about that until the following spring training when I ran into Cal in Orlando. He's one of those guys the minors—and the majors—are full of: the fans never hear about 'em, but they have a big impact on many players' careers. Cal's always got baseball stories about the forties and fifties. I'd tell him, "Cal, I was born in 1961," and he'd go right on with his story from 1947. Baseball. Always talking baseball. In Orlando we hugged and slapped backs. Then Cal leaned in and whispered, "I told you right, didn't I?" I stopped for a minute. I didn't know what he was talking about. Then I remembered his prediction! And I started yelling, "Yeah! Yeah! Yeah!" Everyone stared at us, but nobody but Cal and I knew what the heck was going on. It was our private celebration.

The minor league career that ended in Old Orchard Beach began two years earlier in Elizabethton, Tennessee. The Twins sent me to that rookie ball team after signing me in 1982. Only one flight a day from Chicago on Piedmont Airlines could get me in there. My coach in junior college told me I'd tear up rookie league like it was high school, and that's what happened. I hit .382, won the batting title, and stole forty-three bases. Doc Gooden was in that league that year. I don't remember how I did against him, but I'm betting it was pretty good. I had 105 hits in 65 games. Randy Myers, Vince Coleman, Terry Pendleton, and a lot of other good players were also in that league. It was a famous crop of big leaguers, and we put on some games for the few fans who showed up.

I started off playing center field but then played mostly left field because the organization decided I had a "left field" arm. In other words, not that strong an arm. That surprised me because I'd worked a lot with "long toss" since high school, building up my throwing arm. After that rookie year with Elizabethton I ran into my high school coach, James McGhee, in a bowling alley in Chicago and told him what the Twins organization was saying about my arm. He laughed and said, "Don't worry. Your throwing is the best of your abilities. They'll see." Coach McGhee was right. I led my league in outfield assists the following year.

The minor league people watch the rookie league players very closely. Most of the kids—I was one of the older players at twenty-one—haven't been away from their families much, haven't lived in some stranger's house at "home" and in motels on the road, haven't traveled for hours and days on buses, and most of all haven't played baseball day after day after day. If they were watching me, they found someone a lot quieter than I am now. I'd done well in amateur ball but this was pro ball, a whole different animal. I would say that I was cautiously optimistic about my baseball prospects. I was confident of my ability, but so many things can happen in baseball, as in life.

Our general manager that year in Elizabethton was a guy named Carmen Dugger, who did everything he could for the players. His sister, Irma Dykes, always had a couple of ballplayers staying in her house, and spoiled them. (I wasn't so fortunate. The apartment I shared with a couple of the guys was the "roach palace," completely overrun with insects when we came back from a road trip.) Rookie ball in general is (or was) set up like a family because, in those days at least, almost nobody had any money, and everybody helped out the best they could. Since I was twenty-one and had signed for a little cash—$20,000—I was automatically one of the leaders of that team. Just about everyone else had signed right out of high school for almost nothing, and had to scrape by on the $600 a month wage.

Our favorite fan was a guy named Larry Riddle. We called him Moe. He came out to all the games, gave us pep talks, and asked us to hit one in the pool—the swimming pool beyond the right field fence. He wore the Twins uniform, ran around the bases during the seventh-inning stretch, and slid safely into the plate. We tried to get him to quit the sliding, because he was an older guy and not very athletic, but he kept on. In 1988, the year the All-Star game was played in Cincinnati, Carmen Dugger drove up from Tennessee and was trying to get through the guards in the hotel lobby to see me and Hrbek and Gary Gaetti, those of us at the game who had been through Elizabethton on our way to the majors. The guards were giving Carmen a hard time. The first we know about it is when we see him standing on a chair waving his arms trying to get our attention. We asked the guard to let this guy through, and that's how we got the latest news from Elizabethton. He reported that Moe Riddle was doing fine.

After the season in Elizabethton, I went to my first Instructional League, in Clearwater, Florida, that fall. That's where I first met Cal Ermer and Tom Kelly and Rick Stelmaszek. I was struggling early on down there, so about the third week or so I shaved my head. I'd tried it before with good results. Cal took one look and said, "Uh, oh! You'll get going now."

I'd worn my hair cut short my whole life, practically, all the way back to when my mother took me down to the local barbershop. When I started playing baseball I'd get it cut real low, almost bald, the first game of the season. Various roomies usually did the honors for me, free. Mike Moreno did an excellent job that year in Instructional camp, complete with razor. The Lou Gossett look. It wasn't a superstition or anything, just tradition. Plus it was something for the guys to talk about on Opening Day, when they're nervous. The Puck's hair or the lack of it: a conversation piece.

Strangely enough, Stelmaszek, one of our coaches now with the Twins, has another story about how I got hot with the bat in that first Instructional camp. His version goes something like this: When he showed up at the camp a few days late, Tom Kelly, who was managing my team, asked Rick which guys he wanted to see play. Rick had just met me and was intrigued by my fireplug body, and he'd watched me hit in batting practice, so he said, "Puckett."

"Okay," Kelly said, "but he hasn't done much so far."

"Well, I'd like to see him anyway."

And starting that day I was on fire, as Rick remembers it, hanging out line drives all over the field. I don't know whether that was the exact timing, but I did play really well most of that six-week camp, which was good timing because that was the first time most of the Twins' upper echelon had seen me play.

Then there's another possibility behind my success at that camp: the tattoo. The players got paid every two weeks, and that's when my roommate Moreno and I would go shopping for groceries. To get to the supermarket we passed this tattoo shop. One day I told Mike I'd always wanted a tattoo. He said, "No, you're just joking," and I said, "No, I'm serious." So he called my bluff: "Well, there's the place. Show me something."

It wasn't exactly a dare, but I really did want a tattoo, so in we walked. The artist-in-residence asked what I wanted and I realized I hadn't thought about that. When I did, nothing came to mind but my name. The job took fifteen minutes, cost eight dollars, and I walked out with KIRBY on my left biceps. And I started hitting *hard*.

The following February, the coaches and managers and minor league bosses at spring training had to choose between sending me to the Twins' "low-A" team in Wisconsin or "high-A" team in Visalia, California. After one good year in the minors I thought maybe I was something of a hot commodity, and I was even more optimistic about my prospects when they sent me to Visalia for 1983, telling me if I could do the job there, I should be on my way. I was also shifted that year from left field to center, permanently, I was told, in order to take advantage of my speed. I was just glad that the rap about my not having a good enough arm for center field had been laid to rest, maybe.

However, I started off in right field at Visalia until the regular center fielder got in a fight during a basketball game and got punched in his eye. It swelled up badly. He had to sit down, and I took his place. Then when he came back, the guy in left field started complaining about where he was playing, so they switched him over to right field and me to left. I played all over—left, center, and right—without complaint.

For the life of me I couldn't see how complaining at that stage of my career would do me any good. I just wanted to get *better*, and I was always amazed to see guys—and there were quite a few—who caused trouble for themselves by complaining about this or that.

One of my pals that year at Visalia was Alvaro Espinoza. He's from Venezuela, and his English in the beginning was pretty much restricted to baseball matters. "Espi" did fine with the language on the field, but needed a little help in restaurants and stores. I'd semitranslate for Espi and he would semiunderstand. But then he learned the language fast because he wanted to. It's easy teaching people things when they want to learn.

One night Espi got a call from his wife back home in Venezuela announcing that he was now the father of a baby boy, José. He was excited but disappointed that he couldn't be there, so a couple of us anted up and threw a little party in our four-room apartment in a small complex. Around eleven o'clock the police showed up. They knew we were ballplayers celebrating something, but asked us to turn down the music because our neighbors were complaining. We did turn it down but I guess not low enough, because the police came back and this time they said shut it down or spend the rest of the night in jail. That was an easy decision, and the only run-in with the police I've ever had.

Fairly early that season I had the first even semiserious injury I'd ever had. I pulled my left hamstring running to first base. It was pretty bad, but I played the next few days anyway, favoring that leg, and sure enough I ended up pulling the *other* hamstring. I played all year with both of them wrapped up tight.

But that didn't bother my performance. I hit .314, with

nine homers, ninety-seven RBIs, and forty-eight stolen bases, and I threw out twenty-something guys from the outfield. Three errors. Then I had another solid Instructional League that fall in Florida, hitting around .350—a meaningful figure, because the pitching in that league is just about as good as at any level in the minors, and the players are all legitimate major league prospects. We worked hard all morning on drills and skills and then played games in the afternoon. The coaches told us the first day, straight out, "Hey, this ain't no damn vacation. We didn't pay for you to come down here and sit on the beach. You're down here to work and get better." We did fundamentals like crazy, and if we had a bad day, we'd keep doing them. I didn't mind. I loved it. There were only about twenty guys in that camp, so it was hands-on coaching.

One of the main things they worked on with me was perfecting my bunting and getting a good lead off first. I was really fast and already a good bunter, and I was going to be on first base a lot, they hoped. Plus if you establish the bunt the third baseman has to come in a couple of steps and becomes vulnerable to a sudden shot down the line or between shortstop and third. I knew Rod Carew had added many points to his batting average with real bunts and threatened bunts. At that time I didn't really imagine myself as a power hitter, and I don't guess the Twins thought of me that way, either. I had hit three homers at Elizabethton, then nine at Visalia in about 550 at-bats. The idea of Kirby Puckett, power hitter, came a couple of years later.

In 1983, playing for Visalia, I had the best stats in the Twins minor league organization. MVP in that California League. I read the Twins' magazine carefully and I knew how my numbers compared to all the other prospects', and I'd done really well in the Instructional camp, so I thought for sure the Twins would invite me to the major league camp in Orlando, Florida, for the following spring, 1984, instead of sending me back to the minor league camp in Melbourne.

But they didn't. George Brophy was running the Twins minor league operation then, and he called me at my mom's apartment in Chicago to tell me that he was really sorry, that I'd had a great year at Visalia, but he couldn't invite me to the big league camp because he had other players he had to "protect." According to the rules, which are complicated, and I don't know them all, anybody at that time who'd been in the minors over three years could be drafted by another team unless he was placed on what's called "the forty-man roster" early in the year. Since I'd been a pro less than three years, the Twins didn't need to use one of their forty spots to protect me. No other team could steal me.

George Brophy explained that this decision had nothing to do with the Twins' opinion of my future with the team. After I'd been promoted to the majors and was playing well, George was quoted in the newspaper saying that he also didn't want me in the major league camp that year because he thought if Billy Gardner saw me play he'd want to keep me then and there, and George just didn't want to rush me and maybe spoil everything. After all, my total pro experience had been one year of rookie ball in Elizabethton, one year of A-ball in Visalia, and two Instructional Leagues in the fall. Not all that much. On the other hand, I knew that Kent Hrbek, Gary Gaetti, and Frank Viola, the up-and-coming stars on the Twins, had all sped through the minors and skipped Triple-A entirely.

I didn't figure that I'd be going to the majors in '84. I just wanted to go to the big league spring training camp to meet all those guys. I was in awe of them, and I wanted to be one of them, if only for six weeks. I thought this was a privilege I had earned with my play.

I also knew that the major league camp in Orlando was a *whole* lot better than the minor league one, about an hour away. We minor leaguers called our field in Melbourne "The Rock." Enough said. There were no facilities at all, believe me. It was terrible, absolutely terrible, but one thing I did learn from that experience was to forget about the conditions and play the game. (Now the Twins have a new combined camp in Fort Myers, and it's the envy of the league.)

In any other organization, I would have been invited to the big league camp. I know that. I understand the Twins' thinking *now*, but at the time I was really upset. I looked at some of the players the Twins ended up inviting to that major league camp—Keith Comstock, Greg Field, Kevin Flannery, Larry Pashnick, Dave Baker, Barry Evans, and Frank Eufemia (a pretty good right-handed reliever)—and I just knew I was as good as they were, or better. My reaction that spring just goes to show why so many young baseball players are insecure. Your future in the game, no matter how well you play, is in somebody else's hands until you make the majors. And then it still is, most of the time.

But I'm no good at holding a grudge, so after George Brophy talked to me and my mom, I was just determined to go out and have a good spring and a good season. I tore the cover off the ball from the first day down at Melbourne. In fact, I've almost always had good springs because I think they're important. I play hard from the first day in March, taking extra batting and fielding, because I want to be ready on Opening Day. These guys who always seem to have a slow

April and May—Ryne Sandberg with the Cubs is one—put a lot of pressure on themselves the rest of the season. Rhino can pull it off, but I want to be hitting .330 on May 1.

Of course, it was hot down in Melbourne, even in March, and I think that helped me a lot, coming from Chicago. The heat in Florida helps loosen the muscles. Otherwise, I don't like hot weather. You won't find me lying around on some tropical island in January. I live in Minnesota in the off-season, and always will. I vacation in the land of ten thousand frozen lakes.

There was some interesting politicking going on that spring in Melbourne. I was to be assigned to either Double-A or Triple-A for the season. And it seemed to me that two of the minor league managers were fighting over my services. Charlie Manuel, who managed the Double-A team in Orlando at that time, tried to "hide me" in some games when we were going with split squads. He'd put me in the game nobody was going to see. Other times, he'd be obviously joking when he offered me the keys to his '65 Mustang to take for a ride during the game. Stuff like that. But Cal Ermer also wanted me on his Triple-A club in Toledo—the famous Mud Hens. I was happy that the managers thought highly enough of me that they wanted me on their teams, but I didn't like being stashed away like a piece of jewelry. I just wanted to play baseball.

Charlie Manuel is now the manager for Cleveland's Triple-A franchise in Charlotte. Charlie and I got along fine that spring, but some of the players didn't understand him or some of his coaching methods. He had played in the majors and also in Japan, and he'd say, "This is the way I used to do it." A lot of young ballplayers are pretty uptight to begin with, and when Charlie's method didn't fit theirs, they got upset. Frustration is a common hazard with a lot of baseball instruction. The coaches have their way, you have the way you've been doing something for your whole life, and maybe they're not quite the same.

Charlie liked home runs. He liked to see you swing hard just in case you hit the ball. Guys told me that when he was coaching from the third base box during his Double-A games, they'd look down to him for the sign and he might pretend he had a telescope and was looking way out over the fence. That meant: Hit a homer. One reason Charlie liked me was that I was a hacker at the plate anyway. I didn't have any method. He knew I'd be up there swinging.

Charlie loved to hit baseballs, too, so after the players' BP I'd throw to him for twenty minutes or however long he wanted. We got along great, and did whatever there was to do in Melbourne, which wasn't that much. No one but me drove Charlie's '65 Mustang. Sometimes we'd wrestle in the clubhouse—a pretty fair match, with neither one of us being very big, but strong, nevertheless. Charlie was always trying to get rid of his excess belly, and after I got to the majors I sent him what we call a "fat belt," an elastic band that you wear around your belly to help hold everything in. He pretended to get really mad about it, but we were always teasing back and forth.

One afternoon at The Rock, however, I wasn't teasing. When Charlie threw BP, he peppered the other players with comments and advice. Do this, do that, keep your head down, keep your shoulder in. But he never said a word to me. Not a word. Finally, that afternoon, I got mad and asked him why he never gave me advice like he gave everyone else. I sincerely thought I was being shortchanged. He pulled me aside and said, "Puck, you don't need no help." That's how he always talked, real country. "You can hit, man. You don't need no help. Some of those other guys, they need more help than I can give them." He didn't say this where those players could hear him, but I guess he was right. After all, most minor leaguers never make the majors. I didn't bother him anymore about ignoring me.

At the end of that spring I wasn't assigned to Charlie's Double-A team. I don't know the ins and outs of how they made the decision, but I do know Cal Ermer was respected as a judge of talent and how to move it along, and I ended up going to his Triple-A team. I would miss Charlie, but at least I got a raise to $900 a month!

I know that Cal believed the move to Triple-A for a month was a good one, giving me a taste of better pitching than I had seen in the California League. They say in baseball that if you succeed at Double-A you can succeed at Triple-A. It's a little hard for me to judge that one, because I never played Double-A, but I do know that the jump from A to Triple-A, like I did in 1984, is a big one. I roped about fifteen line drives in my first fifteen at bats during the season. But then . . . sliders! I saw a lot of good sliders for the first time. And no more fastballs right down the chute on 3-and-0, 3-and-1. Hitting leadoff again (I'd led off in Elizabethton), I was expecting the pitchers to come right after me. The idea is to keep the leadoff man off base. But right away I felt they were pitching *around* me. Pitching me tough. Started seeing a lot of breaking balls. Sliders! I'd always been a free swinger with a tendency to help out the pitcher by going after some bad pitches, and nothing's tougher to hit than a hard slider a foot off the plate. I swung at a few of those. Man, it's gonna be tough from now on, I thought. I just really hadn't been prepared for the change. If Cal Ermer told me about Triple-A pitching, his advice didn't sink in until the pitchers started snapping those sliders right over the outside corner at the knees. Then it sank in.

After that really fast start I cooled off considerably, but I was making the adjustment and hitting the ball okay when I got the call to Anaheim and went four-for-five in that first big league game. But it's not unusual for a player to do better in the majors than in Triple-A. You're excited, you're energized, and, like Cal told me in the hotel in Old Orchard Beach, Maine, the lights on the field are better and you can afford three squares a day. When I jumped to the majors my pay jumped, too—from $900 a month to forty grand a year. I was a happy young man.

Of course I knew that pitchers are a different breed, but I got my first real lesson about *how* different from my roommate that first year in the majors, Eddie Hodge, one of the Twins' starters. Eddie and I got along fine except for the nights before he pitched. Then he was so nervous he drove me crazy. About one o'clock I'd wake up and he'd still be watching television. "Eddie, please," I'd complain. "I need to sleep. *You* need to sleep." A couple of hours later I'd wake up again as he was shuffling a deck of cards under the table lamp, starting another game of solitaire. "Hey, *Eddie*. We gotta sleep, man!" Those were long hours for both of us, and enduring that scene every fifth night taught me a lot about pitchers. They're fragile, man, fragile! I felt sorry for Eddie, and that year turned out to be his only one with the Twins.

Ron Washington became a close friend that year, and we were roommates the following year. We had met in spring training in '84—at the major league camp I wanted to be invited to, but wasn't. One day I went over to the major league camp anyway, to get away from The Rock and to try to round up some shoes and gloves and whatever from the various reps. That's common practice among the minor leaguers. I told Ron that very day I'd see him soon in the big leagues.

The Twins thought I could learn a lot from Ron Washington, and I did. He was the oldest guy on the squad, at thirty-two. He's now manager of the Mets farm team in Columbia, South Carolina, and all I can say is the Mets have at least one great minor league manager. We talked mostly baseball for hours. When I might get a little negative, which wasn't very often, Ron was always positive. And that's one reason I try to be the same way with rookies now. It's the standard "If you don't belong, you wouldn't be here" message, but it still helps to hear it spelled out for you personally.

Occasionally Ron thought I would give the pitchers too much credit, if I was struggling. The pitching was better than I'd ever faced, obviously, but Ron convinced me to focus on *my* hitting, not *their* pitching. That's a really important lesson, and I'm not sure coaches drive it home enough with young hitters today.

It's true that the odds of hitting the ball hard go way down when the pitcher is painting the corner every time—Dennis Eckersley, say—but the hitter has to stay positive and think about what he can do to make adjustments. You can't be passive at the plate. That's death. I learned a lot from Ron Washington about being positive, being aggressive, never getting the idea that things at the plate are out of my control. Once the ball leaves the pitcher's hand, *I'm* in charge. That's my theory. That's why I never get involved in discussions on whether some pitcher is doctoring the ball. I have no idea and no concern. Some pitchers do load the ball up with something, or scuff it up—Tim Leary was caught red-handed, and the Twins' own Joe Niekro was suspended in 1987 during our pennant drive—but as a hitter, it's negative even to think about it. Makes no difference to me. I couldn't tell even if they do doctor the ball. The split-finger fastball is just as nasty as any spitball, anyway, and totally legal.

Then again, there's a fine line for the hitter between being in control of the situation at the plate, and blaming yourself too much when you don't get hits. That can also be a hard attitude for young players to learn. Ron helped me get that balance.

He also made me realize that over the long haul of a major league schedule, as opposed to the shorter minor league season, you can't go to the park three hours early and just hit, hit, hit. At that time I still wasn't certain I could hit major league pitching consistently, so I was out there hacking every day at three-thirty. Ron made me realize that regular batting practice, with maybe some extra but not *hours* worth, was all I needed.

He also urged me to change my eating habits. I'd always been a one-meal-a-day guy, maybe two meals, and neither one was breakfast. If I could stay in bed all morning, I'd do it. Ron always made me get up and go out with him for some bacon and eggs. I didn't have to eat anything myself, and if I wanted to go back to bed after that, fine, but he made sure I got out of bed the first time. I went with him, but not even Ron could force me to eat breakfast, and I didn't. I still don't.

I was sad when Ron left the Twins in 1986 because he taught me most of what I knew at that time about being a *major league* ballplayer, instead of just a ballplayer. He taught me how things should be done on and off the field. I'd always sit next to him on the bench and be treated to a running commentary on the play of the game. If a guy had poor form or lousy hustle on the field, Ron would say, "Don't play like that." He was that blunt. I had tremendous respect for him because as a utility guy, he'd go weeks maybe without ever playing. (That's one thing about the game that has changed during my career. Everybody on the team is given a lot more playing time now, especially under Tom Kelly.) After starting at shortstop in '82 and '83, Ron was on the bench in '84 as the Twins went with Lenny Faedo at shortstop. But Ron didn't get down on himself. He was ready when he was called on. He worked hard and stayed in shape. As he often said, baseball was in his blood. By example, he taught me so much it was unbelievable. Every rookie needs a Ron Washington.

He even helped me get my shoes. Ron had introduced me to a couple of the equipment reps in spring training, and when I was promoted to the Twins and started off pretty well these guys were throwing their stuff at me. I didn't sign with a shoe company. I just collected their stuff. At end of the season I had three laundry bags stuffed full of shoes and sweats. Teammates teased me about all the stuff I accumulated. Some anonymous troublemaker pasted the nickname SHOES above my locker. No problem. If you're going to dish it out, as I've been known to do, you have to be able to take it, too. That nickname didn't stick, anyway. (I don't know why, but the situation with shoes is totally different today. Young guys coming in are lucky to get one pair of shoes unless they already have a contract, although if you do have a contract the money is much greater than back then. I wasn't shopping for money, anyway. I was just interested in the merchandise, the nice sweat suits, nice gym shoes for my family and friends. I ended up signing with Adidas for four years, and then switched to Nike.)

One of the standard teases on that Twins team was the white mask, or hood, awarded anyone who struck out three times in one game. I won it in Texas that first year. In baseball terminology, a "K" is a strikeout, so three strikeouts is three K's—"KKK." That's the way the mask read, and I can see how the outsider might think it's in bad taste. Maybe it is. Ten years later, I've decided I'm going to throw the mask in the trash before the '93 season, but mainly because it's too negative. You get two strikeouts in the game and the next thing you know you're worrying about getting that mask. And if you have the mask, you're not happy but you don't want someone else to get it, either. Who needs that kind of pressure, I've decided. Trash it. The pitchers on the Twins used to have a sombrero they presented to any pitcher who gave up four homers; any hitter who struck out four times also got the sombrero. Bert Blyleven—"Gopher" Bert because he gave up so many homers—finally threw that hat away, and rightly so.

Our first game back home at the Metrodome after the West Coast road trip was the first time I'd seen the place, or any domed stadium, or played on artificial turf. But I never had a problem with the Dome, despite all the criticism over the years. It took a while to get used to Humpball, as they call it, with all the weird hops and *hiiiiigh* hops, but mainly I was thrilled to be in the big leagues. I was also happy that I'd never have to play again at The Rock in Melbourne, Florida.

It didn't take long for me to learn how to turn the Metrodome into a home field advantage. A lot of guys on the other teams wore regular steel spikes to bat—rubber spikes in the field, then switching to steel at the plate. But this artificial turf was really slick, from all the football, I guess. So these guys who wore steel spikes would come around second base real fast. Then, when they left the dirt area around the bag and got on turf again, their feet flew right out from under them. Every time! That's how I got so many assists (16) that first year—throwing behind guys who fell down on a big turn at second base! I never had that problem on the base paths because I batted in my rubber cleats. I didn't need steel cleats because I didn't (and still don't) dig in at the plate. I stay on top of the dirt and hit the ball and try to get out of there as soon as possible. But the big, strong guys who hit home runs have to wear steel cleats in order to dig in at the plate. That's okay, but they had to be careful going around second base in the Metrodome, because I was ready to nail 'em.

One of the most exciting games for me took place when the Twins went into Comiskey Park in Chicago for the first time. I had to round up eighty-nine tickets for family and friends. I recall the exact number. And when my mom came down the aisle to her seat and saw me standing out on the field as a major league ballplayer, well, I knew all the work was worth it, no matter what happened in my career from then on. I was so excited I lunged at everything at the plate. A bad performance, no hits, but I didn't let that ruin the day.

That first year in the majors, I couldn't keep up with the four-for-five pace I set in my first game, but I finished hitting .296, with a lot of bunts. Plus I led the league with those sixteen assists, and I made most of the All-Rookie teams and was third in the voting for Rookie of the Year. Alvin Davis, a first baseman for Seattle, won the award that year, and with twenty-seven homers, he deserved it. My teammate Tim Teufel was just behind me in fourth place.

More fun than all that was the pennant race. We were actually tied for first place in early July with a .500 record, and we ended up at .500 ball, but tied with California just three games behind Kansas City. I really wasn't all that disappointed in the end because here I was my rookie year with my team giving it a good shot. In the minors, or in college or high school ball, there was no comparison to that feeling. This was the majors. I couldn't go any higher. I could only get better. And it just felt so tremendous to be playing hard, and playing well, with everybody watching. I realized I didn't mind hitting before twenty, thirty, or forty thousand fans.

However, one game late in the year almost ruined that whole experience for me. We were in Cleveland and leading the Tribe 10-0, Frank Viola on the mound. A laugher, as we say. But then they started coming back ... and back. Those were the longest innings I had (or have) ever experienced. At some point Ron Davis relieved for us, got into trouble, hit a batter, as I recall, while he was loading the bases, and Jamie Quirk, just about the last guy off their bench, hit a grand slam. The Indians won that game 11-10. I was in a state of shock. So was Viola. We all were. You never forget a game like that, and I thought about it again while watching the Houston Oilers blow their 35-3 lead over the Buffalo Bills in the football playoffs this past winter. I hope the Oilers recover because I'd like to see Warren Moon in the Super Bowl, but it may not be easy. The Twins weren't in the playoffs in '84, but in the locker room after that game in Cleveland it seemed like we were—and had blown the chance.

This was also the year that Calvin Griffith sold the Twins

to Carl Pohlad. Donald Trump had bid on the team, too, promising to keep them in Minneapolis. I didn't really care who owned the team, as long as I got to play. Attendance in the Metrodome in 1984 almost doubled over the previous year. We drew over one and a half million fans and then we got a curtain call after the last game.

After the season I wanted to play winter ball, partly because I could make another $15,000 for three months' play, to go along with the $40,000 basic salary I had earned as a rookie. But the Twins had had a bad streak of injuries in winter ball, and they didn't want me to go. In other words, they wouldn't let me go. They gave me a $10,000 bonus instead. At twenty-three years old, I wasn't complaining, nor was I dreaming about arbitration and free agency and multiyear contracts. I was wondering what the Twins would pay me the following year, 1985, but mostly I was just happy to be in the majors, and to already feel that I belonged.

T W O

The Robert Taylor Homes in south Chicago have been called the place where hope dies. I'm living proof that's not the case, and I'm not the only proof. Robert Taylor is down the Dan Ryan Expressway about a mile south of Comiskey Park. Twenty buildings along a two-mile stretch. Home to about twenty thousand people. The best overall description of the place is just one word. They were—and are—*projects*. And the Robert Taylor Homes in particular now have the reputation of being one of the worst inner-city projects in this entire country. The kids who grow up there tend to be written off as no good, and a lot of them are never expected to amount to anything by their parents, their friends, the press, or by anybody, really.

But I grew up there, and I know that was far from the truth in the sixties. I still think it's far from the truth today, although conditions there are much worse now than twenty years ago. The standard line they give is that you may very well come out of the Robert Taylor Homes wearing a uniform with a number, but it's more likely to be issued by the state prison, not by a baseball or basketball or football team. That reads great, but I resent it. Sure there were gangs around when I was growing up at Robert Taylor, and some of the guys I grew up with are dead or in jail, but a lot of good people lived, and still live, in those "projects," and a lot of good things have come out of those people.

I couldn't have gotten very far by myself, however. I had two parents who loved me and provided for me the best that they could. I rarely saw my father, not because he didn't love me or didn't want to be home, but because he was working two jobs to support our family. Dad had played in the old Negro Leagues and was reputed to be a good left-handed pitcher. But he seldom got the chance to talk to me about that or anything else. He'd leave the apartment at six in the morning and return at noon. Then he left again at four in the afternoon and got home late at night, after I was asleep. The morning job was at a department store downtown. The evening job was working as a supervisor at the main post office. He had Sundays off.

On Saturdays, Dad only worked the morning job at the department store, and he'd buy groceries on the way home at one particular store that had lower prices than the small shops near our apartment. He'd call from the store to tell us he was on his way and I'd meet him at the bus stop to help with all the bags. I also helped Mom with the bags on Fridays, when she did the other shopping. We never had a car while I lived there. Mom and Dad didn't even have driver's licenses. My brothers and sisters got their licenses, but for most of my childhood we were pretty much a bus family, a public transportation family. There was nothing unusual about that in south Chicago.

We always had food and clothes and love. I never went without those for a single day in my life. None of the kids did. I'm the youngest of nine. For the record, my sisters are June,

Frances, and Jacqueline, my brothers Charles, William, the twins Donnie and Ronnie, and Spencer. Spencer was the next youngest, and he's six years older than I am. The oldest, Charles, was born when my mother, Catherine, was fifteen years old.

By the time I came along, or shortly after that, only Spencer and Jackie still lived with our parents in our three-bedroom apartment on the fourteenth floor at the corner of State and 43rd Street: 4444 South State Street. We had plenty of room in Apt. #1410.

None of the kids turned out to be hoodlums, but that doesn't mean we didn't have our share of problems. We did. Although not much from me. My mom was determined that the baby of the family would stay out of trouble. I was sheltered. I didn't hang out. I didn't even go to many movies. At night, I was home. It's as simple as that. Baseball and school, that was it, that was my whole life. School let out at three-fifteen, I was home by three-twenty-five, three-thirty at the latest. I'd race in and change, grab something to eat, and be ready to go. But Mom would always ask about homework, and I'd have to do my math or whatever before she let me go play ball.

I played baseball every way I could, every moment I could. My mom, like most mothers, was always saying, "Don't play in the house." I'd play anyway, usually using some balled-up aluminum foil, or socks rolled real tight and wrapped with tape. I became a master of the sock-ball. It was a pretty good ball. My best friend came over and we'd hit and throw. We broke some stuff and I got a few spankings. I must admit I deserved every one.

Outside, we painted a square on the wall of the building to mark off a strike zone. You could see them all over most of the buildings, and almost all those boxes were way too big. In that "league," the high fastball always counted as a strike. That's one reason my strike zone today is so big.

We used rubber balls that cost ten or fifteen cents apiece. I had an allowance of one dollar per week, and with that I could buy two rubber balls and seventy or eighty pieces of candy. My friends lasted till the candy ran out!

The buildings at Robert Taylor were far enough apart so that any fly ball that hit another building on the fly was a long shot, so we called that a home run. One bounce before it hit the wall was a triple, two bounces a double. We usually had one pitcher and two fielders. There was no such thing as a ground ball out. We had a complete system depending on how many players showed up. And we could always depend on at least one player—me. Sometimes we had four or five guys, but if we had more than five—enough for an infield, sort of—we'd go over to a nearby asphalt field (complete with painted bases) and play with a hard ball. And I slid into those "bags" in my shorts.

I could entertain myself just by tossing the ball up and hitting it against the wall, pitching against the wall, whatever. The people who lived there didn't mind these games, but the janitors did and when they came after me or us, we had to take off running. They were trying to grow grass, or so they said. But, hey, what about all the football games played on those "fields" in the fall and winter? No grass ever had a chance to grow there! But that didn't stop the janitors, so we always had to keep one eye on the ball and one eye out for them.

That's pretty much how I played baseball until I went to high school. There was no Little League at the Robert Taylor Homes. When the weather was warm, during the summers,

I'd be playing somewhere by eight o'clock every morning and wouldn't come home till sunset. Even then, I wouldn't come home until I heard my mother's voice calling from the fourteenth floor, "Kiiiiiirby! . . . KIRBY!" I might be playing against the wall of a building two or three buildings away from ours, but I could usually hear her calling. I can still hear her calling now. Occasionally I would ignore the call, but not often. If by some chance I didn't hear her, somebody would come and tell me, "Hey, Kirby, you'd better get home. I hear your *mother* calling you." You know how embarrassing that is for a kid.

When the streetlights came on, the Pucketts knew where they had to be. All of 'em. I could stay out on the balcony on the fourteenth floor after dark, but not down on the ground, because that's where the problems were. That's where the gangs hung out. We heard some pistol shots, but nothing as bad as I hear it is today. Anyway, I was upstairs. I've said that some of the kids I knew are dead or in jail, but those kids weren't close friends. I didn't have many close friends outside the family.

When I was twelve, and the only Puckett kid still living with my parents, the family moved out of the Robert Taylor Homes and into a better apartment on 79th Street and Walcott, an integrated neighborhood. I made a few more friends there, and on Friday and Saturday nights we'd get together at someone's house and eat pizza—always pizza—and watch basketball games on television. At that time the drinking age in Illinois was eighteen, and when we turned eighteen Mom told me and my friends that if we were going to drink any beer, she'd rather we did so in her home instead of out on the streets. She was the first of our parents to allow this. Maybe her attitude sounds liberal, but she was really just being protective—as usual! Seven or eight of my friends from that neighborhood are still good friends. Four of them—Mike Jones, Darryl Hughes, Torrienti Phillips, and Toby Lipscomb—were in my wedding.

I didn't get into any kind of organized ball until I went to Calumet High when I was fifteen. But the neighborhood pickup games I played must have done something for me because I was a high school All-American playing third base. And I got good coaching there, from James McGhee. We worked real hard on hitting the curveball, concentrating on watching the ball all the way from the pitcher's hand. To achieve the effect of a major league curveball, Coach McGhee cut a slice out of a baseball so it would curve a lot in any kind of breeze.

I always thought I had what it took to be a ballplayer, but the scouts never came to see us play at Calumet High School. They were scared to death to come to our neighborhood, and I can't honestly blame them. We didn't even have a real field. No fences. If you hit a line drive in the gap, just keep running. Lots of inside-the-park homers, you might say.

My brothers played ball, too, but none got scholarships or anything, so they couldn't pursue the game any further. They may have been good, but they just didn't get the opportunity. They all went into the Army instead. And they helped me by pushing me to be as good as I could be. They urged me to play ball with guys bigger and older than I was, and so I did whenever I had the chance. I'd just squeeze into those games, and I was usually good enough to hold my own. When I was in high school I was invited to play in summer games on teams with guys four and five years older. I played a lot with a semipro team that had some of the best players in Chicago. Black, white, brown, we had the best. We were officially called the Chicago Pirates, but more informally the Askew Pirates, because Roosevelt Askew, who owned a pool hall and had money, put together that team. This was when the Pittsburgh Pirates were into their "We Are Family" stuff, and had all those different uniforms—pinstripes, white, black, and different hats, too, round, flat, and so on. The Askew Pirates also had all those different uniforms. Six or seven combinations. Awesome. I played for them whenever I wanted to. I'd just call and say, " 'Kew, I want to play today," and he'd tell me where the game was.

I guess some scouts did see some of those semipro games, and I know they were there for the annual south side/north side high school game. Those were All-Star teams. But the scouts who did see me probably wrote me off as too small. Now I've got the last laugh on all of them. I got a kick when some scout was quoted in '88 or '89 as saying that ten years earlier he'd have been fired for turning in as a prospect somebody who was built like me, but now he could write, "Reminds me of Kirby Puckett."

People have always said to me, You'll never do this, You'll never do that. I say all I want from people is just to give me the chance. I can handle it from there. A lot of that confidence must have come from my mother. The rest of my family, too, but mainly my mother. She always said, "You can do it, Kirby." And toward the end of my high school years she started saying, "You can make the major leagues, Kirby." I believed her. My mom was always positive, positive, positive. I tend to be the same way now. However, Mom was negative regarding football. Her message was simple: "You *cannot* play football." So I didn't, on any organized basis, although I liked to play neighborhood games. Mom permitted basketball and I tried out one year for the varsity team, but didn't make it.

I wasn't the greatest student, but my grades were good. I skipped a few classes, of course—doesn't everyone?—but all I'd do was go to the cafeteria for a snack—until the day I was embarrassed to death by my English teacher. Mrs. Singleton was her name. Her reputation was that she was pretty nice as long as you didn't cross her. Nobody wanted to take her class, however, because she expected a lot from you, starting with *showing up*. One day I was eating lunch in the cafeteria instead of attending her class. Somehow she found out where I was and marched over to the cafeteria and marched me back to her class. I don't remember what she said, but it was enough to make me want to crawl under the cafeteria table. I was this cool guy skipping class, only to be caught in front of all of my friends. I was mortified! I never skipped anyone's class after that. That was one of those minor episodes that become major lessons in life. I wasn't going to let anybody embarrass me like that again. I wasn't going to put myself in a position where someone could do that to me.

After graduation I wanted to take that year off from school, but by the following summer, 1980—after Ford let me go and a temporary job with the Census Bureau ran out—I knew something had to give. I had to get a permanent job or a college scholarship. I tried out at one of the summer minicamps that the major league clubs were holding in Chicago. The one I went to at McKinley Park, not far from Comiskey Park, was basically for high school players, but anyone could go to the camp. You could even sign a minor league contract by playing just one game, if you had a really good one and it didn't look like a fluke. My contact at the camp was Art Stewart, local scout at that time for the Kansas City Royals. He's now their director of scouting.

What a zoo! Hundreds of guys, it seemed, were milling around at the park, and the scouts and coaches running the show divided us up among six diamonds, ran us through some drills, then set up teams for games. This went on all day, ten o'clock until dark. I played third base, my position at the time, and got some hits. Art Stewart came over and we talked for a while. Then Dewey Kalmer, the coach at Bradley University, stepped in and introduced himself and said out of the blue, "I've checked your grades and you graduated with a B average. How would you like to come to Bradley University on a full scholarship?"

I was just shell-shocked. Didn't know what to say. I started to say "Yes!" but then decided I'd better go talk to my mom and dad. I jumped in a buddy's car and he zipped me home and I burst through the door and told my parents about the offer. They started crying and maybe I had tears of joy, too, I don't remember.

"Really?!" they said.

"Really?!" They couldn't believe it.

But it was true. They told me to accept that scholarship and go to college. I was ready. The year before I hadn't wanted to go down to Miami because, as I explained, that was too far from home, but Bradley was in Peoria, Illinois, just two and a half hours on the bus from Chicago. I thought if something went wrong back home, I'd be close enough to get back. Bradley was perfect.

I learned later that my small stature was one of the main reasons the Royals and the other major league teams who had seen me play didn't draft me out of high school. My speed they could see and measure, but they could also see my size: I only weighed about 155 pounds at the time. How were they to know that I would put on so much muscle in the pros? Nor did I have anywhere near the arm that I have now.

In short, I was not a "can't miss" prospect in the eyes of the scouts. I was just a regular prospect, and they're a dime a dozen, literally. And I must have felt that way about myself because I did go to work for Ford, instead of taking whatever baseball opportunity came along. At that time, I definitely didn't see baseball as my *inevitable* future. Art Stewart refers to Freddie Patek with the Royals as another "little guy" who defied the odds and succeeded in the big leagues, but I'm willing to bet I was always twice as strong as Patek. *Twice* as strong. But the truth is I might have signed a contract right out of high school and never made it past A-ball. Maybe I needed that year off to grow. Call me a late bloomer. I'm not complaining about the way it all turned out.

Like I said, there are lots and lots of good high school baseball players, and you may need a big break, or several of them, to really get somebody's attention. Dewey Kalmer gave me one of those breaks when he offered me the scholarship to Bradley. Even his presence at that minicamp in Chicago was lucky. Normally, college coaches aren't allowed at those camps, because the coaches are in competition with the major league teams for players. I understand it can get cutthroat. But Dewey had been invited to the camp by Stewart.

If you ask Dewey today what he saw in Kirby Puckett thirteen years ago, he'll say running speed, bat speed, average arm, and one other thing: overall strength. Dewey believes that strength is the common denominator in great athletes, and he thought I might have that kind of strength. He thought right. Maybe he knew that I could—and still can—

dunk a basketball. But he'd also say I stepped into the bucket at the plate and couldn't hit the breaking ball, only the fastball. But the main thing is, whatever Dewey saw in me at the time, whatever he says today, he took the chance on Kirby Puckett.

I took the Greyhound down to Bradley and Dewey met me at the station. The dorms were overcrowded that fall, so I ended up sleeping on a big piece of foam on the dorm floor that first night, along with some other players. This wasn't my idea of college, not even on a scholarship. The next day I told Dewey I wasn't sleeping on the floor anymore. I moved into some kind of bunk, jammed in with some other guys. I didn't want to be rude, but this just wasn't going to do it, either. So I asked Dewey to give me my housing money and meal money and I could find my own place to live. He agreed, and I went out and found a place to live with two or three other ballplayers. That was a nice duplex with a working fireplace, a first for me, and just half a block from the Bradley campus.

But less than a month later, my dad died. I got permission from Dewey to stay home as long as I needed to, and I stayed for three weeks, maybe a month. My mom was my main concern. I wanted to take care of her. I was the baby, my brothers and sisters were all gone from home, so I figured it was time to step up and show what I was made of. While at home I said to her, "I don't want to go back to school, Ma. I'm going to stay home and take care of you."

Her reply was quick: "You're going back to school. I've got too many gloves and too many bats and balls invested in you. Plus you're something special. You're going to make it one day."

She really said that, and I remember it clearly. So I went back to Bradley while she stayed by herself in the apartment on 79th Street in Chicago.

Baseball at Bradley was a disappointment at first. Dewey Kalmer had told me that I would play third base. That was fine with me; that's what I wanted to play. But when the games started in the fall, I wasn't playing *anywhere!* It turned out that Dewey had an all-senior infield. I may have been naive, but it didn't take me long to figure out that I'd never play on a regular basis that season. The best I could hope for was some work in the late innings, mostly pinch running. And I did that well: ten-for-ten in stolen bases to help win some games. Nevertheless, that limited role was not what I had in mind, and after a late-night discussion with my roommates about the situation I got up the nerve to go to the coach's office. Maybe I shouldn't have expected to play that year, I don't know. I didn't understand much about the way the world works, that's for sure, but I was mad. Maybe I was out of line that day, but I went into Dewey's office for a man-to-man talk.

I said, "Dewey, you gave me a baseball scholarship. You told me I was going to play third base and I get here and you've already got an all-senior infield."

He agreed that things hadn't worked out like he'd planned—I forget his detailed explanation—and he said he'd think about the situation overnight. The next day he came over to me in practice and asked if I could play the outfield. I said I could play anywhere he put me. *Anywhere.* He hit me some balls, I caught them, and there I was—a center fielder. This was the first time I'd ever played in the outfield on any official basis. Dewey proceeded to give me a crash course in the fine art of playing fly balls.

There are times in life when you have to stand up for yourself, and that was one of them. I could have sat on that bench the whole year. But I wasn't about to do that without a struggle. I was at Bradley to play baseball, my mom expected me to play baseball, and I was going to do everything I could to play baseball. By the time the spring games began, following the cold-weather layoff, I was starting in center field and I led the team in home runs and stolen bases. I hit about .400 and drove in fifty or so. I was batting ninth in the lineup in some of those games, too. Didn't have a clue how to get a base on balls, but I still did okay. One doubleheader I was on base eight or nine times and I felt pretty sure that some of the scouts on hand that afternoon were watching me as well as the other players.

I made All-Missouri Valley Conference, but I left Bradley after that season anyway. My grades suffered because of my three-week absence and I would have had to go to summer school to be eligible in the fall. I didn't want to do that, and more important, I just didn't want to be so far away from my mother in Chicago.

There were no bad feelings when I left Bradley. I sincerely thanked Dewey Kalmer for how he'd helped me. Dewey helped me in particular with my major problem back then: pulling off the ball. He put a spare tire around my neck, resting it on my right shoulder. It sounds really weird, I know, but the tire in that position kept my left arm and shoulder from flying out of sync. Try it and you'll see how it works. Dewey listened when I talked, and I did the same. Dewey is still the coach at Bradley, and he runs a professional program. I understand that at some colleges the baseball coach just dumps the bats onto the field and rolls the ball out to the mound and says, okay, go play nine. Baseball is often secondary to football and basketball, but it wasn't and isn't that way at Bradley.

Dewey would tell you today that Kirby Puckett was a hungry ballplayer at Bradley who wanted it bad, but who wasn't that good yet; not a lot of polish. I wouldn't disagree. He would also inform you that he nevertheless told a scout the year I played for Bradley that this Puckett kid would turn out to be a great major leaguer, and the scout laughed.

The summer after I left Bradley I played ball in the Central Illinois Collegiate League, a semipro league, and that's when another of those breaks some of us need came my way. The story is pretty famous in the Twins organization, and the tale as it has been passed around is generally true. Stories often change over the years, but this one has stayed right.

This was 1981, the summer the big leagues were on strike. The ballplayers didn't have an agreement and decided the only way they were going to force one was to walk off the field. I didn't follow events all that closely because the majors seemed so far in the future for me at that time. But I did want them to start playing again. The good news was that most of the organizations were pretty much shut down, in order to save money, so Jim Rantz, a scout for the Twins, had the chance to go watch his son Mike play a game in this collegiate league.

Jim and his wife and their other kids drove down to Peoria, Illinois, only to learn that Mike's game was in Quincy instead. So they drove to Quincy.

I was on the other team that night and had a good game—homer, couple of other hits, stole a couple of bases, threw a guy out at home. And I was hitting about .400 at the time. Jim, who's now Director of Minor League Operations for the Twins, told me later that I also stood out as just about the only player on either team who wasn't dragging. It was really hot and there were about twenty people watching the game. Not a lot of excitement in the stands or out on the field, I guess. I didn't know Jim, and he didn't talk to me that night, but he started keeping up with my stats that summer, and put my name in for the Twins to select in the winter draft in January 1982. I was their first pick in that draft, and the third in the country overall.

By that time I had enrolled at Triton College. After I had left Bradley I got in touch with the coach at Triton, Bob Symonds, because I knew they had an excellent baseball program—even the ball field was impressive—and the school was almost right in Chicago. I had met Bob in high school at a tryout camp on their football field, but he was running a makeup baseball game at the time and didn't get much of a chance to see me play.

When I called him, I told him my situation, how I'd done at Bradley, and he said, sure, come to Triton. He met me at the train and set me up with a roommate, David Boston, brother of outfielder Darryl Boston. David and I stayed in the attic apartment of a house owned by a single lady with two sons. The rent was low, and that was good because I didn't have much money. I worked in the laundry room for close to minimum wage. It wasn't the Ford Motor Company, and I didn't get overtime, but I was playing baseball.

So I was playing at Triton when Tom Hull, a representative for the Minnesota Twins, approached me to negotiate a contract after they'd taken me in the January draft. He had been scouting part-time for the San Francisco Giants in the Chicago area while he was an accountant for an oil company. When he retired from that job, the Twins had an opening and hired him. He already had a track record with them. He had recommended Jeff Reed, who became a good catcher. But he had never seen me when the Twins assigned him to negotiate a contract with me and my mom.

Tom Hull came over to my mother's apartment a couple of times, took us out to dinner once or twice, treated us like royalty. It was fun—sort of. I wasn't talking a lot at the first dinner. My mother was doing most of the talking, but when Tom mentioned a $2,000 bonus to sign, I interrupted right there and said, "Two thousand dollars! I worked for the Ford Motor Company making two thousand dollars in a month! Come on now, really!"

I thought he was joking around with that offer, but he was serious. That was my first introduction to how things work in professional baseball. Mr. Hull explained to me and my mom that teams don't give that much money in the January draft. And that was the truth. They don't even have the January draft anymore because there aren't really that many players eligible. Even then, the theory must have been that if a team could sign a player cheap out of the winter draft, fine, but otherwise wait until the June draft to try again. I said I understood all that, but no thanks to his offer. We're not going to sign for two grand. Never.

A couple of days later he calls and says let's try again. He said he'd talked to "the man"—George Brophy—and had a better offer. This time he took us to the best steak house in Chicago, and Chicago has a bunch of them, I now know. He jacks up the offer to $6,000.

"Six thousand dollars!"

Still no way. I had had a real good summer season and then a good fall season at Triton. Scouts were always hanging around that school and I thought I was getting to be well known by now. Being picked third overall in that January draft only helped. I was confident that if I had a good spring season, I'd be drafted again in June. I wasn't worried about passing up six grand.

So I told Mr. Hull no thank you. According to George Brophy, Mr. Hull still hadn't given up, and was planning on setting up yet another meal with that stubborn Puckett kid and his mother. In fact, when the phone rang at Brophy's house about six-thirty one evening not long after the second failed dinner, George thought it might be Tom Hull reporting that he had finally signed me. But it was a woman's voice and she said, "Mr. Brophy, you don't know me but I'm Tommy Hull's daughter. Daddy went out today to shovel the sidewalk before he went to see that youngster and while he was shoveling the sidewalk he had a heart attack and died."

True story. My mother felt badly about it. I couldn't believe it.

Somehow we soon heard—I forget the details—that the Twins were still interested in me but would now wait until after the junior college season. That was fine with me because Triton turned out to be the best baseball experience I'd ever had. In the first place, we were good: just about a 60-10 record by the end of the year. We rarely lost. Our *intrasquad* games in the fall were competitive. We had maybe ten guys drafted off that team in the first three rounds the following summer. Lance Johnson and I are the only ones still in pro ball. Lance is now the center fielder for the White Sox.

We worked for all those victories. We practiced in the snow after shoveling off the football field. Bob Symonds had us take infield practice from the warning track! That's what I call "long toss," and it's one reason, maybe the main reason, my arm is so strong today. We worked on bunting for hours, and the results of that became clear for the rest of my career. Bob was a disciplinarian and he's the most responsible of all my coaches for the way I play today. I learned all the fundamentals from Bob Symonds. He was one of the best baseball coaches I've ever seen. And I could talk to him about anything, anytime. He'd come to wherever I was, if that was necessary. He made it clear to each of us on the team that not everyone, not even every really talented player, can be a professional ballplayer, but he guaranteed that when we left his program we'd be better people than when we went in, no matter what career we chose. I think he was right.

Some of the scouts who had seen me in the summer league thought I should be back in the infield—second base, maybe. I guess they were still worried about my size. I shouldn't have listened to them because I knew I was an outfielder, *maybe* a third baseman, but young players listen to everybody, and that can be a problem because everybody's got advice—different advice. Even the fans in the stands have advice. I told Bob Symonds what those guys had said about second base and he said, "Okay, we'll expose you in the fall at second base." A couple of weeks of that and I realized I wanted back in the outfield. As soon as I told Bob that, he said, "You're out there as of today," and I've stayed in the outfield since.

At Triton I also started to get a little more confident off the field, bantering with the guys, keeping them loose. I'd always been something of a comedian, and at Triton we had a lot of fun. I had 'em in stitches one afternoon teaching the new bunting style I had just invented. It's hard to describe in words, but I'll try. I put the bat right in front of my face, and then drop it out of the way at the last moment, pretending to let the ball hit me in the face and bounce out in front of the plate for a perfect bunt.

Well, maybe you had to be there. Anyway, I was just a

jokester, always had been. I had the whole team crying that afternoon. I don't know why it was so funny, but they were dying laughing. Bob Symonds, Lance Johnson, they all remember that episode.

I also got a reputation on that team for shining my shoes. I wanted to look professional. Scouts were watching. Plus I'd always loved shoes and Mom told me to take care of the ones I had because we only had so much money. The habit carried over. I'd take my spikes home after the game, wipe the dirt off, polish them up. I took care of them like they were dress shoes. The guys looked at me like . . . but, hey, I enjoyed shining those shoes, and mine lasted a lot longer than theirs. Pretty soon everybody at Triton was shining their shoes. It built up our pride, and pride builds a club. I still take care of my shoes and carry an iron with me on the road, too, and iron my clothes every morning. People tease me. "You make plenty of money, Puck. Send 'em out!" Sure, I could afford it, but I like to iron.

Baseball highlights that year at Triton? After the regular season we went to the Junior College World Series in Grand Junction, Colorado. Our first game was scheduled for eight in the morning against Seminole, Oklahoma, another really good program. I was amazed when 5,500 people showed up. I led off and hit a drive to right center and was standing on third base with my arms folded before the throw got back to the infield. The fans loved it, I loved it. Our outfield of Lance Johnson and Dave Boston, platooning in left field, Larry Jackson in center, and Puckett in right caught everything hit our way.

The crowds soon came over to our side in that tournament. We came in fifth and lost the crucial game on a fluke. We were playing some team from Waco, Texas, and the game was tied in the bottom of the ninth, bases loaded. Late afternoon. Their guy hit a high fly that Lance lost in the sun. Nothing he could do. Nothing we could do. They won 5-4.

I was on fire the whole tournament, eleven-for-sixteen, four triples, four doubles. That's still the record for hitting in that tournament. For the season I hit .472 batting leadoff, 120 hits in 69 games, 16 homers (4 in one game), 81 RBIs, 48 stolen bases, and I threw out 20 or so guys from the outfield. I was at the top of my game back then, and was voted Junior College Player of the Year for our region.

Probably the greatest catch I made that year was down in Tennessee. I was playing right field that night, and playing pretty shallow because Bob Symonds had been working hard with me on that—playing shallow and firing home or to third. So I was shallow and right center field in that park was really deep. Their guy hit a long, long fly with the winning runs on base, I think, and I just ran as fast as I could as long as I could, and I caught the ball over my shoulder just before I got to the wall, going away, full speed. Fun, I'm telling you.

People look at me today and say, "You were a *speedster*?!" They say this to my face sometimes. That's an insult, because I'm still sneaky fast legging out a surprise bunt if the third baseman plays too deep, but when I was twenty-one, twenty-two years old, I was really fast. But even then I had to prove my speed.

Coach Symonds, myself, David Boston, and Lance Johnson were riding out to the field. We were talking and Boston asked me how fast I was. I said I ran a 6.3 "sixty." He and Lance started laughing. They couldn't believe I ran that fast. I assured them I did. So we had a showdown on the track. Bob Symonds had his stopwatch handy. Lance and I lined up and took off at Coach's signal. Make that a 6.05 for Puckett—but they said I jumped the gun. So we lined up again and I didn't jump the gun that time and ran a clean 6.3. Then I did it again. That quieted them down. Later I ran 6.45 *uphill*. I was fast, I tell you, *fast*. And the thing that amazed everybody was, I couldn't even touch my toes. I have never been able to touch my toes. This amazes people. I guess my muscles are real tight, but they've never failed me or put me on the Disabled List—knock on wood. (I had to wrap my thighs that one year in the minors, but the closest I came to the DL was in 1990 when I pulled my hamstring in Kansas City and messed around with it for a few days. It hurt again and they sat me down for a week or so until it got well. But no DL.)

One day while Lance Johnson and I were talking about our schoolboy days he realized that we had actually met, and played against each other, years earlier, when we were thirteen or fourteen years old. His team from Lincoln Heights in Cincinnati had gone up to play a team from Chicago. They won the first game too easily and their coaches suggested that the Chicago coaches get some better players. I was one of the new guys brought in for Chicago, and the next day we played a 1-0 game that Lance says was one of the best baseball games he's ever been in. I was pitching (like many kids, I played all over). Cincinnati won. At least, that's how Lance remembers it.

After junior college, I didn't see Lance until 1987, when the Twins played the Cardinals in the World Series. Lance was with them at the time. He came over to my house and we shot pool and listened to music. Back at Triton we had played a lot of cards and pool and I always won. Always. And I won the first three pool games in Minneapolis, but then he came back and won the next three. That's when I decided it was time to do something else, listen to some jazz, whatever. He teases me about not letting him beat me at my own game in my own house. That's right! Now that Lance is in the American League we get to play against each other and visit several times a year. I remember one homer I hit right over his head, a little to the right of dead center field. It was a kick rounding second base and looking out at him standing on the warning track looking at me, shaking his head, smiling.

That year at Triton was a wonderful one in my life, and several years ago Triton had a ceremony to honor me, retiring my number at the school (29), and in my brief talk to the crowd I said again what I'd said before: Coach Symonds had taught me how to play baseball. I didn't think I'd be standing there that day if it hadn't been for him. Then, in another ceremony, they renamed the ball field at Triton the Symonds/ Puckett Field. I'm proud of that. The sad thing is that the first jersey put on display at the school was stolen. I think a second one was, too. Now they have a third jersey, but they're worried about putting it out. This bothers me. If they do display that jersey, I would appreciate it if the souvenir hunters would leave it alone.

After that season at Triton, I was sitting pretty when the Twins came knocking again at my front door in Chicago in June. After all, I was Junior College Player of the Year for my region, and junior college baseball is real baseball. Lance Johnson says that Triton was better than South Alabama, the Division I school he transferred to that missed going to the College World Series by one game.

All of a sudden—in about eighteen months—I'd gone from being a regular prospect at best to something of a hot property. Sometimes the story goes around that if baseball hadn't been on strike in 1981 and Jim Rantz hadn't driven down to

Quincy, Illinois, to see his son play, I might never have been drafted. It makes a great story, but it isn't true. As Jim Rantz said, my numbers couldn't hide. I was just a much better ballplayer, fundamentally.

In fairness to all the scouts who passed me over coming out of high school, and even while I was at Bradley, I had gained a lot of strength since then. I wasn't any taller, but I probably weighed fifteen more pounds. There was just a lot more to see in 1982 than there had been in '80. In fact, I found out later that a rumor started going around with some of the scouts that I wasn't the youngest of the Puckett children, but the second- or third-oldest instead. They decided that the scrawny boy of a couple of years earlier was, all of a sudden, a mature twenty-four- or twenty-five-year-old man. Really! Anybody who knew me at all knew I was the youngest Puckett.

The Twins still had signing rights to me for a few weeks after the end of the Triton season, and the new man they sent in was Ellsworth Brown. He started coming to some Triton games and talked with my mother at some of them. Other scouts were telling my mom that I could go for $100,000 in the June draft, so if I didn't sign with the Twins I could rest easy and go back into the pool for that draft. Of course, some of those scouts might have been telling her that so I wouldn't sign with the Twins and their own teams would have a chance to draft me. You hear a lot of stories about what goes on when scouts are trying to sign ballplayers.

I wasn't thinking that much about money. I'd been reading the papers and I knew that Twins owner Calvin Griffith had dumped just about all his high-priced players after the 1981 strike and was going with a team of young, cheap players. It was pretty common knowledge that Calvin planned to bring these guys up, let them play for two years before they became eligible for arbitration, and then trade them if it looked like they would command a high salary in arbitration. Maybe that wasn't even true, but that's what I read, and it was fine with me because that meant I'd have a chance to move up fast. That's all I wanted. I was on a mission to make the big leagues. That meant much more to me than $100,000. I wanted a good bonus, but even more I liked the idea of moving up fast with the Twins.

In my very first meeting with Ellsworth Brown in his hotel room, he offered me $20,000. So my "holdout" six months before had already made me $14,000! That tickled me. I signed on the spot and naively thought I got the money right then. But that isn't the way it works. More like half now, half later—a year later. I gave the first ten thousand minus taxes to Mom, then the next year when I got the rest I bought a Buick.

1980 Skylark Limited, sixteen thousand miles, brown and gold—used car, man, awesome, and it was all mine. It was my baby. It was the first thing of much value I'd ever owned. I was so proud of that Skylark, I'll never forget it. The guy charged me like six grand for it, a good deal, but I had to pay on a note because I didn't have enough cash after I'd paid the insurance. Living in Chicago, that was $1,200 a year; more than that, maybe. Chicago's crazy. I was under twenty-five, too. Anyway, that's how my finances shaped up back then. When I got to the big leagues I gave the Buick to my sister, and she sold it a few years ago. I should have bought it back, for old times' sake.

T H R E E

On April 22, 1985, I finally hit my first major league homer, off Matt Young of the Mariners. A *shot*, I tell you . . . all the way to the second row of the left field seats in the Metrodome, just beyond the glass, 340 feet from the plate. I was greeted by my teammates with the old silent treatment. They just sat like nothing had happened, and here I had finally hit a dinger after about six hundred major league at-bats. I wasn't so naive that I didn't know about the silent treatment, but a couple of minutes went by and still nobody had said anything.

"Geez, guys, weren't you watching?" I broke the conspiracy of silence myself. "Don't you know the Puck finally hit a homer?" Then they relented after what I felt was an excessive period of time and came around and slapped me on the back.

I hit three more homers in '85, twenty-nine doubles, and thirteen triples. Seventy-four RBIs. My batting average of .288 was a disappointment for me, and I came up one short of two hundred hits. I knew I was closing in on that mark as the season wound down. I was learning that the reporters will let you know about this kind of thing. Now I couldn't even tell you the details of my final at-bats, trying for that final hit.

Some at-bats I remember, some I don't. Some stats I remember, some I don't. But one thing I've never done much is worry about what's done and over. It's useless. I didn't get hit number two hundred and the Twins never climbed back in the pennant race. We finished 77-85, a long way behind the Royals.

I was still a new guy in the big leagues, a sophomore, and I didn't know much about how pro baseball works, but I was learning fast. In early June of '85 the papers reported that Carl Pohlad, our new owner, had assured our manager Billy Gardner his job was safe despite his team's slow start. Two weeks after that vote of confidence from the owner, Gardner was fired.

In the minor leagues, they don't fire managers during the season, as a rule. In the majors, it almost *is* a rule. I knew this, of course, but that first experience was still a shock. We were picked to win the Western Division that year by a lot of writers. We were young and gung-ho and pretty good, and the Western Division didn't have a real powerhouse. But we just weren't delivering the goods on all our potential. By mid-June we were seven or eight games out, and when the players don't perform the manager gets the blame. That's just the way it is, as everyone knows, but I'm not sure that the fans realize that players sometimes feel bad about this situation. Five years later, when the Twins had such a poor showing in 1990, when nothing was going right and we ended up last in the division, we were worried that Tom Kelly's job might be in jeopardy, and no one wanted to lose him, especially since what was happening—and not happening—wasn't his fault at all.

The newspapers decided that Gardner's problem had been

that he tended to wait around for the big blow from Hrbek or Brunansky. And they said he wasn't a great communicator with his players. We generally heard from the manager through the press. Billy once called motivation a "college word" he didn't understand. But his main problem was that his players weren't winning. The funny thing about the motivation issue was that in order to get the team going, Billy got himself kicked out of a game the night before he was fired in Kansas City. His scheme worked. We came from three runs back to win. A lot of good it did him. Of course, I liked Billy Gardner because he took a chance on me the previous year, and when he came in the clubhouse the afternoon he'd been fired to clean out his locker and say good-bye to everyone, he wished me good luck and said he'd be watching my career. I appreciated that. I think he really meant it.

Our new manager, Ray Miller, had been the pitching coach for Baltimore. Apparently he was hired after a one-hour interview in an airport hotel somewhere. Ray had never managed at the major league level. But he was a pitching expert, and the Twins wanted better pitching—of course.

Toward the end of that '85 season, when it was obvious we were going nowhere despite the change of managers, one very interesting thing did happen to me. A lot of my 199 hits that year had been to right field. A *lot* of them. I'd always had an inside-out stroke, taking the ball to right field. Like I say, I was a singles hitter. During a batting practice late in the season the guys were teasing me about being just a right field hitter and not being able to hit home runs. I'm not sure why I reacted, because I basically agreed with them, but I decided to accept the challenge. I don't remember saying anything

like, "Oh, yeah, I'll show you!" but I proceeded to hit about
ten home runs in a row. Bombs, too, not fly balls into the second row just beyond the glass. I'll bet that word of that BP
session spread quickly through the Twins organization. It
gave everybody something to think about. It gave *me* something to think about, and the following spring brought a dramatic change in my hitting stats.

1985 was also the year that the drug indictments came down
in baseball. That summer the Twins signed Steve Howe, who
had a well-publicized problem with cocaine. Steve had been
released by the Los Angeles Dodgers early in the season, but
the Twins needed pitching and took the chance. Steve was a
good left-hander. But he hadn't been with our club long
before he turned up missing one weekend in Cleveland in
September, right after he'd appeared on "Nightline" to discuss
drugs in baseball. The team had unspoken fears, naturally,
and two days later Steve admitted that he had backslid and
asked to be released from the club. The Twins were glad to do
it, and then declined to give him another shot in the spring. I
think the common emotion shared by everyone in baseball
was sadness that guys were hurting their careers and their
lives. We were also concerned about the reputation of all the
rest of us in the game, because only a very small percentage
of players ever used drugs. That spring almost all of the Twins
agreed to drug testing, at the request of the management. I
was all for it, but some of the Twins and other players around
the league thought the issue should be handled through the
Players Association.

The drug problem in baseball seemed relatively inconse-
quential compared to the problem at the Robert Taylor Homes

in Chicago. The combination of these baseball episodes, my background in Chicago, and my increasing visibility in the Minnesota region made my wife, Tonya, and me decide that we wanted to do something to help kids stay away from drugs. We became involved with "Drug Free Minnesota," a program run by Skip Humphrey, the Attorney General of the state. The idea is to give kids something else to do, and not just to preach to them to stay away from drugs. They participate in different projects, such as putting together public service announcements about drugs. These projects earn points for the school, and whichever school gets the most points wins tickets to a Twins game and a big picnic outside. The Twins provide the tickets.

Tonya and I go around to the different schools during the winter. I do most of the speaking, but Tonya does her part as well. We try to sell the program and encourage the kids to get involved with it. But mostly I tell them about my own background because that's the best way I know to make clear that drugs aren't necessary. I may be locally famous now, and have plenty of money, but a lot more important than all of that to me is my family. More important is being good at what I do and proud of what I do. More important is that I've become successful against a lot of odds—not terrible odds like a lot of kids face today, but bad enough that I know what those kids are going through. My dream has always been to play major league baseball, and now I am living that dream. All it took was believing in myself, and a lot of hard work. I try to convince the kids that they can live their dreams, too.

My contract for my rookie year had been the standard one-year deal at $40,000 plus the $10,000 bonus the Twins gave me instead of allowing me to go to winter ball. After that year, a pretty good one, I had expected some kind of raise for 1985, but I had no leverage at all. Arbitration was two years away, in my case. But the Twins gave me a big raise anyway, all the way to $120,000 plus $10,000 in incentives, more than they had ever paid a second-year player. That was fine. The only problem was that I had to adjust to the fact that, from now on, my financial standing would be public knowledge and a subject of debate. There's nothing I can do about that, but I still don't like it.

After the 1985 season I hired Ron Shapiro, an attorney and agent who lives in Baltimore and represents Cal Ripken, Jr., Eddie Murray, and a lot of the big names in baseball. Eddie, who was a friend by then, told me I should meet Ron, and toward the end of the '85 season Ron and I were both in Cleveland and we ran into each other in the hotel lobby. I was getting change from the cashier and Ron was passing through. We just hit it off immediately and came to a quick agreement shortly after that first meeting. I knew who the strongest agents in the business were, and Ron was one of them, but one of my main considerations in going with Ron was that I didn't want my negotiations on the front page, and that is Ron's style, too. If you're vocal you can get your teeth kicked in. Ron doesn't go in for a lot of public confrontations. I think my choice was about the best move of my life. The owners and general managers respect him. Ron always refers to himself as a positive-energy person, and I guess that's what I am. That's how we work together. He's also my good friend.

Ron got into our business by accident. One of his first jobs out of law school was as Maryland's Securities Commissioner, working to uncover fraudulent deals. This was in the seventies. The Baltimore Orioles asked Ron to investigate some schemes that had cost their hero, third baseman Brooks Robinson, most of his savings. Brooks was so impressed with Ron's work that he asked Ron to be his agent, and later to help keep some of the other players out of trouble. The rest is history, and Brooks is now part of Ron's staff of experts.

I have total trust in Ron. If somebody wants to talk business—and they all seem to want to talk business—I say, "Fine, talk to my agent, Ron Shapiro. He lives in Baltimore. He's a Harvard Law graduate. He used to investigate crooked deals. Here's his phone number." (I don't tell them they have to get past Ron's secretary, Gloria, but they find out.)

I immediately appreciated his work for the 1986 season because I got a raise to $230,000 plus incentives. And Ron still had no real leverage in negotiating. All he could do was prod the Twins to pay me what was fair. After starting out at forty grand, plus the bonus, two years earlier, I was really happy. I was also happy to learn that Ron lived on a farm with a variety of animals, including peacocks, and an excellent little pond where the bass are always biting. Now, when the Twins go through Baltimore during the season, I get out there as often as possible. I'm on the water at 5:30 A.M. and off before the sun gets too hot.

After the hassles of my ballplaying life, fishing is very relaxing for me. You can just go out there and forget all your worries. Everything goes blank. You hope you're talking to the fish just right so they'll jump on your hook. Sometimes I get in some fishing with my father-in-law. He has a little eighteen-footer we take out early so I can be home before noon. And a few times a year, definitely in spring training, a whole gang of Twins goes out on a lake somewhere. I've gone out on the Gulf of Mexico off Florida—caught an alligator one year!—but I prefer fresh water. The biggest fish I've caught was a seven-pounder in Lake Erie, just last year. Now that seven-pound walleye is mounted on the wall of my study.

I do not own a boat. I can't see the sense of paying good money for one and having it sit in my garage. Not now, when I'm playing ball. I work all summer! But a year or two before I retire I'll probably get a boat, when I'm on my way out of the game. I can't say I'm looking forward to that retirement, but I'm not dreading it, either. A summer all for myself and my family? Sounds nice to me.

F O U R

When my future wife Tonya's Aunt Leslie wrote down my license plate number before she let Tonya and me go for a ten-minute drive, I knew this was a pretty cautious family I was getting involved with. Fine with me. I respect that attitude.

Tonya gets embarrassed when she tells people that we met in a nightclub, because she is not a nightclub person at all. Most evenings back then—1985—she stayed home and watched TV with her parents. But that night in the middle of the baseball season, her sister Nicko and her Aunt Leslie and a few friends were going out to this restaurant/nightclub, and they talked Tonya into going along. The restaurant was upstairs, dancing was downstairs, and I was downstairs with John Butcher, a pitcher, and a couple of other buddies from the Twins. We were talking and joking around when Tonya and her group came in, and she just caught my eye. I waved to her and she kind of waved back, embarrassed-like. A while later I caught her eye again and gestured for her to come over to me. That surprised her, and I don't think it made her all that happy. She had an obvious "Give me a break!" expression on her face. But I can be persistent and somehow I talked her into walking over to our table—without saying a word. Probably flashed my biggest, most charming grin.

That's how we met. She introduced herself as Tonya Hudson, and I introduced myself as Kirby Puckett.

"Nice to meet you."

"Nice to meet you."

And so on. It was clear she didn't know who Kirby Puckett was. Ballplayers complain about all the fan attention, but we're also surprised when we go unrecognized in our hometowns. And I was having a big year! A big year! So I added, "Kirby Puckett of the Minnesota Twins." Maybe that rang a little bell for her. She did know who the Twins were, and now maybe the Puckett name kind of fit in. But to this day she still teases me about saying "Kirby Puckett of the Minnesota Twins." I guess I deserve it.

We talked for a while and I learned that she worked at a jewelry store and as a supervisor at a clothing store, and had just quit a third job because it was too much. Both remaining jobs were downtown and she was riding the bus back and forth to her home, leaving early and getting home after nine o'clock. She lived with her parents. And like I said, most nights she spent at home with them.

She said she was not a baseball fan *per se*. I remember the "*per se*." I get to tease her about that. Sometimes she's still not a baseball fan *per se*. One night a year or two back I got in the car after the game and she said, "Nice game, Boo." That's her nickname for me. I said, "Nice game?! I went 0-for-4, struck out twice, and we lost! What's so nice about that?!"

I also learned pretty quickly, if not the night we met, that Tonya had given up on men for a while. We were "jerks."

I took her over to introduce her to John Butcher. And I

spontaneously said, "John, this is my new girlfriend, Tonya Hudson." She gave me a look, you can believe that. I was surprised I said it myself, but I meant it, too. Then I met her sister and aunt and the rest of that group. I asked her sister if she'd like a drink and Nicko replied, "No, you don't have to buy me a drink. I have my own money." But when she fished around in her purse she couldn't find her wallet, and finally said, a little embarrassed, "Well, I guess you can buy me that drink, after all." We all laughed about that.

Fifteen minutes later I was telling Tonya she was going to be my wife. I felt that way. I'd never said anything like that to any other woman. The "give me a break" look reappeared. Tonya thought I was just feeding her a line.

By now the place was closing and I offered to give Tonya a ride back to her Aunt Leslie's, where she had left her own car. That offer brought on a serious discussion, I can tell you. Should we let this guy drive Tonya to get her car? Look, I said, I play for the Twins. The cops would catch me in a second if anything happened. And that's how Leslie ended up taking down my license plate. Not only that, she gave me *ten minutes* to get her niece to her house. If I wasn't there, she was calling the cops. True story.

I drove to Tonya's aunt's place pretty fast. And I told Tonya again that she might think this was crazy but she would end up being my wife. I took down *her* number—her phone number—so I could check that she got home okay, and I asked her out for lunch the next day. Night game, you know. And I guess I told her one more time that she'd be my wife because she delivered a little lecture.

"You know," she said, "if you marry someone you should be in love with that person. I don't know you, you don't know me, you don't know what I'm like. I could be crazy. So you shouldn't keep on saying that right now. Do you say that to *everyone?*"

This time she believed me when I said I'd never done anything like that before in my life. I'd had dates, of course, but no one very steady. I was twenty-four years old that summer. Tonya was twenty-one. We made a date for the next afternoon and had lunch downtown. After a few of these dates she decided I wasn't such a jerk and was even worthy of meeting her mother. Tonya's mother worked downtown at the gas company, so we met near there for sandwiches. We met at one of the Arby's and I just had a Coke but wanted to pay, of course, because I thought that was my responsibility. Mrs. Hudson didn't want me to and she won that dispute. She reminded me immediately of my own mother. We just hit it off and now she sometimes joins the guys for card games at my house. The Hudsons have four daughters, no sons. I'm considered the son they never had.

Then finally it came time to meet Tonya's father and the rest of the family. They set it up for a Sunday afternoon when Tonya was going to be at work. She'd join us later. One o'clock sharp, and I was there. Mr. Hudson was working in the front yard when I strolled around the corner and we introduced ourselves and the rest of the Hudson family poured out of the front door. Just about all Mr. Hudson said to me was, "Man, I could never have done this." He still says that, but I've never had any problem getting along with people, so it was no big deal for me.

I'm not much of a cook, but I have picked up a few specialties over the years, and one night after I'd been dating Tonya a couple of months I decided to prepare my excellent beef Stroganoff for all the Hudsons. I cooked the meat at my place and took it over to their kitchen, where I did the noodles and sauce and everything. It was an informal affair, with Tonya's family sitting around chatting while I finished up in the kitchen.

When we started eating, nobody said anything. "Great, isn't it?" That was me talking. They didn't say a word, and I only found out later they thought it was the worst beef Stroganoff they'd ever had. Shoe leather. They had to force it down, they said. That hurt.

Perhaps I should have fried catfish. That I can do well, I promise. Catfish is my usual contribution if Tonya asks me to cook some evening in the off-season. Unfortunately, she doesn't like fried catfish, but I think of that as her problem, mainly. I fry catfish anyway. Tonya's specialty is fried chicken, red beans, and rice—black heritage food, as she calls it. That's usually what she cooks if some visiting ballplayers are coming over for a meal after a game. Reggie Jackson loves it. So does Bo.

On September 26th I proposed to Tonya. We knew we wanted to get married the following year. I gave her a nice diamond ring and then blasted a long one in the game that night. Twins won—although it was too late to help that season.

The next season, 1986, was even worse than '85 had been. We finished twenty games under .500, twenty-one games behind the California Angels, and barely ahead of Seattle in the cellar. For me, however, that was a big year, a brand-new experience, because I started hitting home runs on a regular basis. In fact, I'm still the only player in major league history to have a season with no homers in at least five hundred at bats—my rookie year, 1984—but then to come back in a later season to hit over thirty homers. I had thirty-one in 1986. That changeover from a singles hitter to a guy with more power started in earnest in spring training.

Tony Oliva was the roving hitting instructor for the Twins while I was in the minors, the guy who'd come into each minor league town for a week or so, work with the hitters, then move on. He had the whole team's confidence, and he had mine especially because Tony and I hit the ball sort of the same: inside-out swing, no great power, hit for high average and score runs. But even back in the minors Tony had suggested that I had the body and the power to hit twenty homers a year. I was bigger than Jimmy Wynn, after all, the guy they called the Toy Cannon in Houston, and a player I had been likened to around the league. He had hit more than twenty homers year after year in the Astrodome, a much harder park for home runs than our Dome in Minneapolis. But I knew there was a big difference between Wynn and me: He held his hands way back from his body and had a real long swing. I could never hit like that. If that's what it took for homers, no thank you. I just laughed when Tony had said I could hit a lot of homers. Yeah, *sure*, Tony. Plus the idea scared me. Being known as a home run hitter brings a lot more pressure. I didn't know whether I wanted that.

But late in '85 I'd hit those ten in a row in batting practice to shut up the guys who'd been teasing me. I used my regular swing that afternoon, and concentrated on pulling the ball if it was on the inside half of the plate. Still, in real ball games I automatically thought, "hit it hard anywhere for a base hit." I didn't think, "home run." I was very comfortable putting the ball in play and using my speed. At the same time, I knew I had more power. I just didn't want to mess up my basic stroke trying to hit homers.

Tony had explained to me how hitting for more power could actually help my average. The outfield would have to play me deeper, and they couldn't depend on me to hit the ball to right field. They'd have to spread out, therefore more holes. My average might actually go *up* if I added power to my repertoire.

So in the spring of 1986, going into my third year in the majors, I got serious about hitting for more power—pressure or no pressure. I had lifted some weights in the off-season, and by then I had the confidence to experiment in spring training. Tom Kelly believes that a ballplayer needs about five hundred at-bats in the majors before he really understands what he can and cannot do at the plate. I needed all those at-bats, and then some.

But changing the style and the thinking of a successful ballplayer is a tough thing to do, as Tony knew. You go three or four games without a hit while trying something new, and that experiment is probably over. I was as open to advice and change as anyone, probably, but neither of us wanted to do anything that would start messing with my mind. One advantage I had, as any hitting instructor will tell you, is that it's easier to take a guy like myself with a natural inside-out, push-the-ball stroke and teach him to pull the inside pitch than it is to take the dead pull hitter and teach him to push the outside pitch. Maybe it's all in the head: the dead pull hitter has that image of home runs in his head, and doesn't want to give that up.

Within a couple of weeks in spring training Tony and I developed my high leg kick, Mel Ott–style, working early every day and late every day. It wasn't easy at first, but I didn't feel that it was hurting me. I could feel it coming around, day by day, and I started hitting the ball hard to left field as well as to right, depending on where the ball was thrown. My confidence got a big boost in one of the early games when I hit a car way out in the parking lot—a police cruiser. I pulled that ball hard but didn't feel I had to overswing to do it.

My swing before that spring didn't have that kick at all. You can check the tapes. I just stood there and poked at the ball. When I hit the ten homers in BP, I poked at the ball *hard,* that's all.

To have a good high leg kick, you first have to shift your weight to your back leg, then transfer that weight forward. If you hit the ball—and even if you don't—everything is going *into* the pitch. Timing is the key with that kick. Tony and I worked day after day on the timing. If you don't do it right you can look real bad. Too early with the kick and you have to hesitate and that won't help. You *might* be able to do something with the pitch. Too late, however, and you're dead. Strike three. Sit down. The timing has to be perfect, but it can't be anything you have to *think* about at the plate. It has to be so automatic that your only idea is hitting the ball hard. Quite a few players have real high leg kicks, including Strawberry, Sierra, some others, but I don't know how many of those guys developed theirs while they were in the majors. Not many, I suspect.

I came out of that spring training camp charged up, full of confidence, and I never lost it the entire season. Tony Oliva had been right all along, but I didn't feel that I could have hit with more power earlier in my career. Everything in its own time. In '86, I was ready. I was American League Player of the Month in April, and led the majors in homers with nine, while batting .389.

One of those blasts was really special. The scene was Yankee Stadium. The first time I'd ever walked out of the visitors' dugout there I almost got chills, and two years later I was still in awe. The place was so *huge*. But this day in 1986 I'll never forget. I'd been hitting the ball great in my first at-bats, but two long flies had been caught on the warning track in left-center. (That was before they moved the fences in.) Ray Miller came up after the second long out and said, "This park's too big for you." I didn't say a word.

Joe Niekro was pitching in the seventh inning, three-and-two count on me, and he threw the fastball knee high. I swung and you could have heard that *Crack!* a mile away. That ball hit the monuments out in center field on the fly. Five hundred feet, they say. All my teammates were jumping up and down on the steps of the dugout, and I was jumping up and down myself. But when Ray stuck out his hand I said, "I'm not shaking your hand. Too big for me, huh?? There's your 'too big.' "

We do a lot of joking and teasing on the Twins, but I wasn't positive that Ray had been entirely joking with his remark to me, so maybe I wasn't entirely joking when I said, "There's your 'too big.' " I'm sensitive when someone tells me I can't do something, as I've admitted. I don't like it. I hit a bomb that day and Ray never bothered me again.

The following Saturday Marv Albert interviewed me long distance for a "Game of the Week" segment on NBC. Marv pointed out that about a hundred more homers had been hit so far in 1986 than in '85. Some people thought the baseballs must have been different, although tests never showed it. Marv asked whether "hot" baseballs were the reason I was hitting homers for the first time. Honestly, I didn't think so, but I told Marv that whatever they were doing with the ball, if anything, was fine with me!

He also talked with Reggie Jackson on that show. Reggie

had commented earlier in the week that the Twins were short of black players. In fact, the Twins had one black player at that point. Kirby Puckett. Reggie had realized this standing around before a game in the Metrodome. He looked out on the field, down the bench, all around, and then said dramatically, "Puck, you're the only brother on the Twins!"

I said, "Yeah, I know, but it's no problem. There'll be some others coming up."

But you know Reggie. They don't call him Mr. Vocal for nothing. He says, "Oh, no, I'm going to say something about this."

So he goes to the press and here come the headlines: REGGIE BLASTS TWINS FOR BEING PREJUDICED. Reggie stirs all this up, then leaves town! All these reporters come flocking to me. I said, "Reggie has the right to say whatever he wants to say. I know I'm the only black guy on this team, but I don't have any problems with the Twins. Not at all." Which was true. And I wasn't alone for long.

My view on racial prejudice in America is pretty simple. Of course it exists, everyone knows that. Every black man and woman can give you story after story about their own experiences. I'm sometimes treated much differently in stores after they see my name on the credit card. Those stories are a dime a dozen. Recently, Tonya's mother and nine-months-pregnant sister were pulled over by a policewoman who drew her gun when Tonya's mother reached into her purse for her driver's license.

At the same time, I've never felt that prejudice put any pressure on my baseball career. For this I can and do thank Jackie Robinson, Willie Mays, Hank Aaron, and other black superstars who paved the way—the hard way. In 1992 while on the road I carried in my bag Aaron's new book, *I Had a*

Hammer. People say Aaron is bitter. Read this book and you'll know why. How can he enjoy memories of breaking Babe Ruth's home run record when many of the letters he received in 1973—the most received by any private citizen in the whole country that year—were threats to kill him or his family?

Hank Aaron was called "nigger" and a lot worse every day that season. I've been called "nigger" just once, by some bigot in the bleachers in Arlington, Texas, several years ago. When I turned around, the coward wouldn't even identify himself. That isolated episode is not pressure on me; it's that guy's ignorance and his problem. Could have happened anywhere. But it did remind me what it must have been like for Robinson and Aaron. There's no way I could ever really know, however, because things have gotten better in this regard. On the whole, baseball and baseball fans are open to black and Hispanic players. If you can play they don't care what color you are—not openly, at least.

Managing might be another story, but I think those barriers are falling, too, with Cito Gaston's success, and with what I *promise* will be Don Baylor's success with the Colorado Rockies. Wait till you see how those guys—whoever they are—play for Don Baylor.

On the other hand, consider the Steve Howe case. Steve has now had how many chances with his drug problem? Seven. Maybe he deserves them, I don't know, but if he were black or Hispanic, would he get that many? No way.

What about front office and ownership problems? This question brings us to Marge Schott. But let's face it: She's not alone in her attitudes in baseball's front offices. I don't know how Schott's situation as an owner will end up, but I do know I wouldn't sign with the Cincinnati Reds. She has a right to say what she wants to, but baseball has the right to choose who should be part of the game at the highest levels—and at the lowest levels. If just half of what Marge Schott has been accused of is true—and she has admitted to using the word "nigger"—she has no business in the game. One poll showed that a majority of the people in Cincinnati supported Schott. The people who called the talk shows seemed to be on her side. I don't guess Hank Aaron is surprised at all.

Baseball has big problems in a lot of areas, but I am not, by nature, a high-profile kind of person. I'm not comfortable getting up on the soapbox like Reggie. It's not my style. You can criticize me for that if you want to, but I am what I am. When I talk to groups of schoolchildren I bring the issue back to a lesson I learned when I was a kid, and that was taught by my parents: Don't let anyone tell you that you can't do this or that, for whatever reason. In my case, I was told I'd never be a ballplayer because of my size. My race was never an issue, to my knowledge. But race does come up in some careers, and I urge these kids to remember that only they know their own talents, and no one can stop them from accomplishing their goals.

I followed that huge homer at Yankee Stadium with a couple of shots in Detroit on the first pitches of those games. It was just unbelievable to walk to the plate and *know* that I was going to hit the ball hard somewhere. The leg kick and the weight work had really helped. Even Paul Molitor, then of the Brewers, a player I really respect, said that my bat speed was noticeably greater that season. I guess it was. Those homers in New York and Detroit seemed like they also brought me a lot more respect from the Twins fans. At the airport in Minneapolis a group of about twenty met the plane with a big sign that read, "WELCOME BACK KIRBY." That was pretty embarrassing—especially when it turned out that most of them were Tonya's family.

As the All-Star game approached that summer, I was in the running to make the team for the first time, and I really wanted that honor, I'll admit it. Don't underestimate how proud ballplayers can be, even when we make a lot of money. We want to be the best, and we want to have it show and be recognized. I'd seen the All-Star game the previous year in the Metrodome and rooted for my man Tom Brunansky. Now I might be able to play in the Astrodome game. But late in June I was still fourth in the voting for outfielders, behind Rickey Henderson, Dave Winfield, and Reggie Jackson. You bet I was watching the totals, and again, if I wasn't the reporters made sure I was kept up-to-the-minute on the standings.

In early July, just before the balloting was over, I was only about seven hundred votes behind Jackson for the third slot. The papers said I had a shot of being the first Twin to start on the team since Roy Smalley started at shortstop in 1979. I don't know whether they knew that I would also earn a $10,000 bonus. So I couldn't pretend that I wasn't thinking about making the team. And I thought I deserved it. I was hitting .340, with sixteen homers and almost fifty RBIs.

But then I fell behind by seven thousand votes and thought I was out of it. So I was overwhelmed when Ray Miller brought me the news that I had won after all. I was sitting on the bench in a game against Detroit. It turned out that most of the votes for me came from outside Minnesota. People had always said that Minnesota teams and Minnesota players never got the respect from around the country that they deserved, and I was happy that my teammates and I would get recognition outside the Twin Cities.

I was on the phone talking with my mom practically every day before the game. I wanted her to share my excitement, and she didn't let me down. And Tonya, whom I would marry in the fall, and my future in-laws came down to Houston for the fun. I was a local hero in Minnesota: About that time Randy Bush teased me that the only way he could get his little boy Ryan to eat the right foods was to say, "Kirby Puckett loves broccoli." Ryan would wolf down his broccoli. I got a kick out of that. I hate broccoli.

In Houston, Dick Howser announced I'd be his leadoff man in the game, meaning I, instead of Rickey Henderson, would have the honor of being the first man to face Doc Gooden. I joked to the writers that if Gooden punched me out on strikes, I'd hope the fans were still out getting their food at the concession stands. If I managed a hit, I'd hope they were in their seats. As it turned out, I stroked Gooden's first pitch—a fastball, naturally—up the middle for a ground ball single.

My real surprise in Houston was that I wasn't nervous at the plate. I was the only American League player to play the whole game. Howser told me afterward that he knew that if he kept me in the whole time, we'd win, and we wanted to win. The American League hadn't taken the All-Star game in three years, and not much in a lot of years before that. And win we did, 3-2. I finished up one-for-three with a walk. Lou Whitaker's two-run shot off Gooden was our big blow.

Shortly after that game I got one of the biggest shocks of my career. Ray Miller called me into his office and said right out front, "You know, Puck, sometimes it's good to hear this directly: Maybe you don't realize how talented you are, how much the other club respects and fears your ability. I'm coming from the other side. I know. I'm telling you, they just don't know how to get you out."

The last thing I expected to hear from the manager were compliments like this. But Ray wasn't through, because the next thing he said was, "Congratulations, kid."

"Congratulations on what?" I don't think I was smiling when I asked. I had no clue what was coming next.

"You're my number-three hitter from now on."

"What?!" I think that's exactly what I said. I was speechless. I thought maybe Ray was playing a game. Baseball is full of people playing jokes all over the place. But he repeated what he'd said. This time I managed two words: *Third, coach?*

I wouldn't have been more surprised if he had said I was batting cleanup. I'd mostly been the leadoff hitter in the majors. In college and the minors I'd hit all over the place, and I'd been moved around a little my rookie year, but basically I now thought of myself as a leadoff hitter, the guy they count on to start things off by getting on base. That had seemed to be the final decision by the Twins organization. And I thought it was the right one. "Batting leadoff, playing center field, #34, Kirby Puckett": That's who I was as a ballplayer. Hit singles, bunt, run fast, steal bases, score. RBIs are a bonus, and somebody else's problem, mainly. Even the reporters were happy that the Twins had finally found a solid number-one man. I was hitting some homers, yeah, but I still thought of myself leading off, like a Rickey Henderson.

But the third hitter is supposed to be the team's very best hitter, and that includes hitting for extra bases, driving guys in not just from second base, but from first, too. I didn't think I was our best overall hitter. Kent Hrbek, Gary Gaetti, and Tom Brunansky were all strong hitters with more experience than I had.

But for the third time Ray repeated that I was now his

third hitter, and this wasn't a request. It started to sink in. Hitting third is a totally different kind of job for a baseball player, and I wasn't sure I was up to it. The previous season I had exactly 4 home runs and 74 RBIs in over 700 at-bats. Well, you could argue that the RBIs were low because I was leading off. Maybe, but the homers weren't low for that reason. I just didn't think of myself as a home run hitter, despite what I was doing that season, and although I had always hit quite a few in college and the minors (where there's no comparison).

I'm not exaggerating when I say how unsure I was about this decision. In my mind, the change they were asking of me was *drastic*. I was finally getting comfortable in the majors, confident of my abilities as a leadoff hitter, and now this. I was honored and scared at the same time.

However, we didn't have much to lose. The Twins were hardly streaking to the top of the division. We were 37-51 at the All-Star break, and I couldn't understand it, because we had better players than that—a lot better. Gary Gaetti was among the league leaders in homers and RBIs, and rookie Steve Lombardozzi at second base was looking at a Gold Glove, maybe. I hoped that the All-Star break would give everyone a rest and we'd come back winning. But this didn't happen, and before we knew it we had yet another manager. Ray Miller had lasted a little more than a year. Tom Kelly took over on September 12, after some talk about Billy Martin coming back, or maybe even Billy Gardner. Martin had won a division championship his only year with the Twins, 1969, and had been fired by George Steinbrenner in 1983, with several years running on his contract with the Yankees. But management passed on both of these Billys.

I think it was immediately clear to everyone that Tom Kelly wasn't just another manager. Six years later, everyone with the Twins will tell you that TK (as everyone calls him) is the best manager the club's ever had, including Billy Martin, and not knocking Martin. TK had been with the Twins as a player and coach for a lot of years, so we all knew him, and vice versa. There wasn't much he could do for us with less than a month remaining in the '86 season, but I clearly remember his little speech at the start of the following spring training. He said we were going to work hard and play hard and do the little things the way they were supposed to be done, and if anyone didn't like that, please let him know and a change of teams would be arranged, one way or the other.

Managers always talk tough in spring training, but the difference with TK was that he really meant it, and we knew it, and he would enforce it. Tom will either earn and command respect from his players or he'll do something else for a living. I really believe that. He made it clear immediately that he didn't care how long we'd been around, how much money we were making, how many years were left on our contracts. From then on, before any Twin would loaf or dog it or make mental errors day after day, he'd ride the pine, as we say. If you don't feel like running out every ground ball, your services will no longer be required by the Twins. TK might put it more colorfully than that. Unfortunately, the trend in the game today is moving in the opposite direction. Too often, in my opinion, you're not seeing the game played the way it's supposed to be.

Frank Viola had seen TK manage in the minors and been

impressed by his managerial style back then. He told me about a game when TK went out to the mound to get the pitcher in the middle of a bad inning. The second baseman on his team took advantage of the break to walk over and start chatting with the runner standing on second base. Pretty soon the two were laughing loudly. After the pitching change was made and Kelly was back in the dugout, here came a new second baseman before a pitch had been thrown. The message: What's so funny when you're getting your butts beat? Nobody loves the game of baseball more than Tom Kelly, and he can't stomach any sign of disrespect for baseball.

Al Newman, who joined the Twins in 1987, also learned a lesson or two from Kelly. Al was really upset after an at-bat and threw his helmet. Anyone who's followed the Twins knows that we seldom do that. As Bob Symonds had taught me at Triton College, don't give the pitcher the pleasure of seeing you get mad just because you made an out. He got you out, that's bad enough. Don't give him any additional pleasure. Great advice. Pass it on. Sitting in the Twins dugout you might hear something break in the runway, but you won't see it happen in the dugout. Myself, I run hard to first base on a ground out, run hard back to the dugout, place my helmet in the rack, and take a seat. Usually. One of the times I did get upset happened to be the moment Rick Aguilera walked into the dugout as one of the newest Twins in the Frank Viola trade in '89. I was storming around in the runway off the dugout when Rick appeared. I politely introduced myself, welcomed him to the club, and then went back to being mad. I must have butchered a fastball down the middle.

But when you get six hundred or more at-bats a year, it doesn't really make sense to let one get to you like that. Many times I've looked foolish for three or four at-bats, only to get a hit in the crucial situation and come out of the game looking like a hero. So you have to think out there before you get mad.

That's Al's belief, too, but this game he did throw his helmet. I don't remember the details, but if I know Al, he felt he had screwed up something basic, like advancing a runner to third on a pitch he felt he should have handled. TK saw the outburst, of course, and immediately went up to Al and said, "I never want to see you do that again. That's not you." Generally, when a guy's upset everyone leaves him alone for a while. Don't risk a nasty confrontation. So now Al was *twice* as mad. Also, he had seen other guys throw a helmet from time to time and they hadn't received a personal reprimand from the manager. So why him?

But then Al realized that Kelly's key words were, "That's not you." That's right, he realized. He wasn't that kind of player. Throwing a helmet doesn't suit him. Maybe Al threw a helmet in 1992 with the Texas Rangers. I don't know, but I doubt it. He never threw another one with the Twins. As I say all the time, if you can't play for a manager like Tom Kelly, you can't play at all.

That story and the impact it had on Al were the kind of subjects we discussed until all hours of the night. We had been good friends from our days in the Instructional League, when Al was with the Expos. We played his team one morning and he was astonished because it was 90 degrees and I had on long sleeves. Plus our uniforms were wool, or at least they seemed like it. Al couldn't figure out why I made things worse with the long sleeves. After the game we discussed this and a hundred other subjects. We were two short guys, both pretty good ballplayers on the Instructional League teams, and we built our friendship from that point. Newman left the Twins after the '91 season to go to the Texas Rangers, and at that time he was my best friend on the club. He's a great guy with a great attitude who happens to be the only player in major league history to play at least twenty-five games at short, second, and third in each of four straight seasons. Al's way beyond being a "utility player," but that's the category he's sometimes put in. A Tom Kelly kind of player: always prepared, always hustling, always smart.

Al had never had a roommate before, even when he was a rookie, but when he came to the Twins I asked him or he asked me to be roommates on the road. So we spent trying times but happy times in the same room. We talked about everything. My mom, his mom, my family, his family, baseball, of course, anything at all. It would often be three or four o'clock in the morning before Al and I realized it. We'd look at the clock and say, "We'd better go to bed!"

The Twins had a group of eight guys who shared doubles. For all those years Gary Gaetti and Kent Hrbek doubled up, even though they could well afford getting singles. (The team pays the price of a double room; if you get a single, you pick up the difference.) Even as late as '91 quite a few of the Twins were doubled up—very unusual. Most guys go single today.

Hrbek and Gaetti also bowled together, and I joined them in a league one off-season before Hrbek developed his rotator cuff problem and couldn't bowl anymore. I got up to a 160-170 average, but those guys were much better. And our reliever Gary Wayne is a fine southpaw bowler. He looks herky-jerky on the mound, but he's smooth as silk on the lanes. Gary can bowl 200 or better, and he puts the ball right on the edge of the gutter with all that spin and brings it back to the pocket. I can't do that. The guys tell me I roll a good ball, but just when I'm getting my average up in the off-season, I've got to go to spring training and hit that small ball. As a rule, baseball players don't bowl during the season. I wouldn't recommend it at all. You don't want to be fooling around with sixteen-pound balls when you're trying to make a living with your fingers and your arm.

Even though the Twins were long gone in the '86 pennant race by then, August 19 was a big night against Boston. I went three-for-four and took the lead in the batting race against Wade Boggs, at .349. And that night Hrbek, Gaetti, and I all had our twenty-fifth homers of the year. I mean, there was no good reason I could figure out why this team wasn't winning more games. Pitching was a problem, of course, but it wasn't that bad.

I couldn't keep up that torrid pace and my average slipped a bit the rest of the way. I didn't stay in the third spot in the lineup, either, but switched back to leadoff most of the time. Anyway, Wade won the batting title that year and he deserved it. I ended up third behind him and Don Mattingly. You have no idea how hard it is to hit .333 for a whole season. I had no idea until 1986, either. At that level, one hit a game is not enough! The jump from being a .300 hitter to a .333 hitter is just incredible. The idea that I was competing against a guy— Wade Boggs—with close to a .350 *lifetime* average was mind-boggling. By the way, I'll bet right now that nobody comes close to .400 again. Boggs is a hitting machine, literally. If he couldn't come close to .400 over a season, as careful as he is selecting pitches, nobody can. Mark it down.

At season's end, playing for Tom Kelly, I was out of the battting race but still found myself in the running for Most

Valuable Player. Peter Gammons in *Sports Illustrated* said, Yeah, Puckett is having the best season in the American League, but his team is not winning, so the nod should go to Roger Clemens, because he was helping his team win the pennant. (That would be the year Boston won the AL East and then lost to the Mets in the famous World Series, with the ball bouncing between Bill Buckner's legs at first base in Game Six.) Ernie Banks defended the idea of voting for the guy enjoying the best season, period, regardless of how his team was doing. Ernie said he was pulling for me. That was especially great for me because Banks is my all-time baseball hero, even though I was more of a White Sox fan as a kid. The Sox played in Comiskey Park, only about a mile from the Robert Taylor Homes.

Ernie won the MVP award twice while playing for second-division teams. And Rod Carew won the award in 1977 when the Twins finished fourth, but they were in the race until September and finished with a winning record. So I knew that the winner is usually with a winning team.

After all the talk about my chances, I didn't even come in second. Sixth place instead, and that cost me some money. Fifth place would have been worth a $25,000 bonus. One newspaper reported that my agent, Ron Shapiro, was mulling an "appeal," since I had come so close. Where do they get this stuff?

I wanted to win, of course, but I wasn't all that worried about the MVP race. I don't worry about stuff I can't control. I don't know where I learned that, but I'm pretty good at it. People seem to be amazed about that part of me. To this day I've never won the MVP award, and maybe I never will, but if I've played my best and somebody plays better, or maybe they didn't play better but won anyway, well, there's nothing I can do about it. However, I do believe in some kind of justice—for example, Cecil Fielder has been rooked. I've never felt that way about any of my own seasons, but I've never hit 51 homers and 132 RBIs, like Cecil did in 1990. If I did post such power numbers—which I never will—I might be upset at being closed out. I'm sorry, but Cecil Fielder should have won the MVP award at least once, if not twice.

Now people talk about the Hall of Fame all the time. They project that I might post Hall of Fame stats before my career is over. I've got no control over that, either. I'll do my job and let the voters do theirs. If they vote for me, fine. Thank you very much. If they don't, I've still got nothing to be ashamed of. Not at all. Maybe that's why I'm so easygoing. I worry very rarely. Maybe I'll have to worry when I die, I don't know!

I don't worry about being the guy at the plate with the game on the line—even though it's not always that exciting when you're up against a Ryan or an Eckersley! It's not easy, but I like that position. Mr. October. Reggie Jackson. That's who I grew up with. Besides, what's the worst thing that can happen? If you deliver, you're a hero. If you don't, you don't. A fifty-fifty shot—not that high, late in the game, when the odds go down low when they bring those relievers in. But I've never been afraid to fail. That's always been a big plus for me. Some guys are afraid to make an error. No. I go for it. If I make an error, I make an error. If I strike out, I strike out. The big hits and the big catches more than make up for those disappointments.

I did win the Gold Glove in 1986, along with teammate Gary Gaetti, and I'll go ahead and say that I thought we both deserved it. I was happy to collect another $10,000 bonus, and I was glad to get some respect for my fielding. Homers are great, but what about robbing other guys of homers? Just as much fun, believe me. The catch everyone now remembers was in the sixth game of the World Series in 1991—more on that later—but I first got a lot of attention with one back in 1985. But I should also say this: If you play the outfield long enough, you're going to get the opportunity to make a bunch of great catches, and if you're any good at all, you'll pull off a percentage of them.

The play that got everybody talking was in July in the Metrodome against Detroit. Ninth inning, of course, two outs, we're leading by two runs and they have two men on. A homer would put them ahead, and Lou Whitaker rifled one out toward right-center. On that kind of ball, you just start running as hard as you can to get into position *maybe* to make the play. I got there in time, leaped up and beyond the wall, I guess, and came down with it. At the exact moment of a catch, it's all instinct. But I was helped along by Bruno— Tom Brunansky, my mate in right field—who had a good angle seeing the ball, and he was screaming, "You're all right! You're all right!" Something like that. Then when I came down with the ball we just went wild. We were falling all over each other, the fans were screaming, the guys in the dugout were jumping around.

By 1986 I was very confident about my fielding. Maybe a little too confident. Even Tom Kelly, coaching at the time, said sometimes I tried to do too much. Ray Miller said you can turn singles into triples in those cases, and he was right. But I thought I could do it all, and nobody was going to tell me any different. I wanted the ball hit to me. Six or seven years later I may have lost a step, but I still want the ball hit to me.

One final note about the '86 campaign, on a subject I get touchy about. At the start of the season, in spring training, there was a lot of talk about my weight. There'd been some talk in '85, too, when I arrived in camp weighing 205-210. People were comparing me to the little guy who weighed 185 pounds his first year. I think I was 210 in '86, and it really accentuated my fireplug look, but that was muscle, man, and muscle weighs more than fat. The Cubs' old Hack Wilson was built a lot like I am, but even shorter and heavier, and that's why his picture is on the door of my locker. Hack lived differently from the way I do—he was pretty wild off the field—but as a hitter, he's an inspiration. In 1930 he hit .356, with 56 homers and 190 RBIs. That's one of those marks that will never be broken or even approached again.

People see me today in my Twins uniform and they say, "Puckett's fat!" If they saw me with my shirt off, they'd know better. Or they could ask Al Newman. I beat Al every year on the fat test the trainers gave us in the spring, and Al's in as good a shape as you can get. It really gets to him that I look like I do and still have less fat than he has. I start off the season at 11 or 12 percent body fat, and I'm down to 10 percent by the end of the season. Anyway, after I hit the thirty-one homers in 1986 I didn't hear any more about my weight for a while.

Because of a change in the major league rules, I still wasn't eligible for arbitration prior to the 1987 season. Ironically, that change came about as a result of the '85 strike. Under the new rules I needed three complete years to qualify, and I didn't quite have that third year. I was in the first group that had to wait three full years. Under arbitration, I would have been able to get around $750,000, maybe more, as the going rate for a player at my level, with my stats. Instead, I was once again without leverage. Even holding out wasn't a realistic option, because the Twins had the right to simply renew my contract at my old level, or even cut it by up to 20 percent. I wouldn't have walked out anyway, and Andy MacPhail, the Twins' general manager, had told Ron he didn't want to simply renew the contract. I had a lot of conversations with Ron over the winter, dozens of hours altogether, because I wanted to be sure he knew my thinking, and I wanted to know his.

I wasn't happy with the Twins' first offer, which was $265,000, a $30,000 raise over my 1986 salary. The fact that the Twins' original offers to Frank Viola and Gary Gaetti included no raises at all didn't make any difference to me and Ron. The newspapers joined us in immediately dismissing that offer. No one, probably including Andy MacPhail, even took it seriously. Not much happened until spring training, and Andy and Ron agreed to wait until another top two-year player signed a deal before proceeding with mine. Andy admitted that, basically, my justifiable salary was being "deferred" until 1988, when I would have the option of arbitration and, therefore, some leverage, finally. Maybe I did deserve the salary of Brunansky and Gaetti and Hrbek, Andy MacPhail said, which was around $1 million apiece, but I would have to wait a year to get it. The Twins finally came up with a second offer, this one for $365,000. Andy told Ron and the press that the Twins' offer would make me the highest-paid regular player in my two-year group, and the second-highest paid in that group altogether, behind Roger Clemens. And Clemens had won the Cy Young and MVP, Andy added.

We were asking for about $425,000. I told the reporters I

didn't think I was being treated fairly. I added that I'd see Andy MacPhail in arbitration the next year. I wasn't nasty about it, just stating the obvious.

One day later, I signed for $365,000 plus $100,000 in incentives. Ron told me it was the best I could do given the situation. And I told the press again that it was all pretty frustrating. I never thought about money while I was on the field, and I was glad the negotiation was over with, but I was also glad that next year I could have some leverage. It doesn't take long as a ballplayer to have sympathy for the old-time players who never got any leverage at all: Here's what we're paying you, take it or leave it. But they couldn't "leave it."

Tonya and I were married on November 1, 1986. We had a medium-sized wedding, but by the time it was all over, both of us wished we'd had a much smaller affair—or, better yet, gone to Vegas! I love the place. Now we try to get out there a couple of times every off-season. Tonya says I'm a cheapskate, but I don't think playing the quarter slots makes me a cheapskate. You can play a long time and have a lot of fun and not lose much money. What's wrong with that? Tonya also says I'm terrible at blackjack. No way. I'm just an *intuitive* player, while she's into the science of the game. If you hold this and the dealer shows this, then you do this. She's always trying to teach me these rules. No. That's not my way. I try to guess what the dealer's hiding.

We had no honeymoon after the wedding because our new house in Brooklyn Park was just about completed. Living in Minnesota full-time was a big decision for me. I had an apartment in Bloomington, a suburb, but I also spent time at my mom's apartment in Chicago every off-season. But Tonya

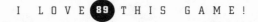
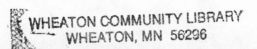

was from Minnesota and she thought it made more sense to settle in Minnesota. She lived there. I played there. It did make more sense.

At her dad's suggestion, I lived in Tonya's parents' house for almost the whole season in 1986, while Tonya and I were engaged and waiting to get married and also waiting for our new house to be finished. When I showed up with my stuff, her mother made a big deal about all the "junk"—her description of my possessions at that time!

FIVE

fter some hassles I had my contract for the '87 season, but that left two bigger questions on Opening Day in the Metrodome. Could I do as well as I had in 1986, and could the Twins do better? In '86, one third of my 223 hits had been for extra bases: thirty-seven doubles, six triples, thirty-one homers. Before that season I couldn't have imagined in my wildest dreams that kind of extra base production. Big-time power hitters can average even higher than one third extra-base hits. Take Cecil Fielder. In 1990 and '91 combined, 45 percent of his hits were for extra bases. But I wasn't in that category. The previous year, 1985, one in four of my hits had been extra base jobs. And now that I'd had the big year in 1986, I knew it wouldn't get easier in '87. TK made it clear in spring training that I was the number-three hitter permanently because we had picked up Dan Gladden from the Giants in the off-season. Danny is the definition of the scrappy leadoff hitter, so they could move me to third and expect me to produce. I would see a lot of change-ups and a lot of breaking balls. I wasn't going to see many fastballs down the middle, that was for sure. If I was going to hit a homer, it would have to be off the pitcher's pitch, not mine. The only fastballs I was going to see other than mistakes were the ones that missed my chin by a few inches—if I ducked fast. Then again, the hitter can always count on the pitchers to miss their spots occasionally and serve up a fat one. Some hitters figure they have a good chance of seeing at least one good pitch to hit in every at-bat. That pitch is a mistake.

Sometimes I'm called a "bad ball hitter," meaning I can handle pitches that aren't even in the strike zone. The opposite is a "mistake hitter," the guy who waits for the mistake down the middle of the plate. I'd say that I'm both of those. I'll swing at anything, but I love those mistakes. Any hitter does, and you have to be ready for them because they can arrive at any moment. The big change in my game in '86 had been that I wasn't afraid to try to pull that mistake over the fence. In previous years, I would have thought, "Ah, here's a big, fat single up the middle." But a pure power hitter is going up there *looking* for that mistake, waiting for it as long as possible—but then grounding out to third when he doesn't get it. That's why I am not and never will be a pure power hitter. I don't want to bat with that kind of thinking. I'm hackin' from the first pitch. A homer is great but a single is fine, too. But now that I was batting third, an RBI was also required.

What about the Twins on Opening Day '87? I looked at our lineup and knew we were a good team. Gladden would play left field and lead off. Tom Brunansky was in right field. I had earned another year in center field. Infield: Kent Hrbek, Steve Lombardozzi, Greg Gagne, and Gary Gaetti. Randy Bush and rookie Mark Davidson would fill in for the outfielders and great utility work from Al Newman in the infield was guaranteed. Catching were Tim Laudner and Tom Nieto. We had hitters who got on base, power hitters, dual-role hitters (me), solid fielding throughout, and guys who played hard every game. We weren't the most glamorous team in the league, by any means, but a down-in-the-dirt, Tom Kelly lineup that should win ball games. My only regret about the new Twins was the loss of old pals Mickey Hatcher, Alvaro Espinoza ("Espi," from our days in Visalia), and my mentor Ron Washington.

Pitching we had Frank Viola, Bert Blyleven, Mike Smithson, Les Straker, and knuckleballing Joe Niekro. And we had Jeff Reardon in the bullpen for the final three outs. He came over in one of the first deals engineered by Andy MacPhail. A team feels a lot better knowing that there's a legitimate stopper in the pen. Now we had him. We also had new Astroturf, the same stuff we played on in Kansas City, and it was thought to be the best. We shouldn't see any more of those ridiculous high hops for which Humpball was famous. And the new stuff was bright green, not faded out. The Metrodome looked pretty sharp and the experts thought the home team looked pretty sharp, too.

I had no idea that we'd go on to win the World Series, but I thought we should be good. Another reason I was pretty confident was the tone set for the team by #10, our new manager. I haven't played under nearly as many managers in the majors—only three—as a lot of guys, but I've decided that managers have it or they don't. I thought Tom Kelly had it.

The season started off with a bang. In our opener in the Dome against Oakland I had a homer, double, and single, and I took extra bases, maybe a homer, away from Mickey Tettleton. With the score tied 4-4 in the tenth inning, he hit a high arc toward the wall in center. The replay showed my armpit above the top of the wall, and that wall is seven feet tall. I can jump, I tell you! Five-foot-eight and I can dunk the basketball . . . sometimes, sometimes not. But I didn't dunk that baseball. I caught it. Tettleton kicked second base in disgust. That was my first standing "O" for the season, and it's nice to start that way, I'll tell you. The dugout was going crazy and somebody kissed me right on top of my shiny new bald head—shaved just for the occasion, of course. And we won in the bottom half of the inning. Then the next night another long one from Reggie Jackson was headed for trouble but I grabbed that one at the fence. I had robbed Reggie the previous year, too, with the bases loaded. Maybe he wasn't too happy with me after those two plays, but that's the way it goes in baseball. Good friends off the field, enemies on the field.

Late innings, guys on base, the hitter smashes a long fly toward the gap in right-center—I tell you, nothing is more fun than playing center field in the big leagues. I've always dreamed of owning some land out in the country that I could roam around on whenever I wanted to, and when I retire I'm going to buy that land, but sometimes I have that same feeling right now playing center field. That's *my* land out there, and don't you go messing with it with your doubles and triples and homers that barely clear the wall. You'd better get the ball way over. I've always said that I'd rather take away a homer than hit one. I really feel that way, and that's the real proof that I'm not a power hitter *per se*.

And the same goes for Danny and Bruno. They didn't want you invading their territory, either, when we teamed up in '87 as the steady outfield for the Twins. We were only together for one year, because Danny joined us in '87 and then Bruno was traded away a year later, but that was long enough to establish great camaraderie in that outfield. I really loved playing outfield with those two guys; I even enjoyed practicing with them. We didn't just stand around shagging fly balls. We made practice like a game situation. Field the ball, spin, throw to a base. We took a lot of pride in our work. When the game started, we didn't even need to call for the ball. At the crack of the bat, we knew whose play it was. We just knew. We never collided. We never came close. One of us almost always caught the ball. Now, I'm sure some longtime Twins fan will remember some episode and hassle me about it, but there were very, very few of them.

After a while that trio hardly even needed to check with each other on positioning the hitters. We shifted not only with each hitter but with the count, and we always knew the other guys were shifting, too. Of course, we looked at each other just to make sure, and checked with TK and Wayne Terwilliger, who handled the outfield from the dugout, but that was usually a formality.

But Danny and Bruno didn't play every single game, of course. One of those other games was a near disaster. It was also one of the biggest laughs I ever had in the outfield. Randy Bush was playing right field that night in Oakland. Bush, remember, is the guy who still teases me about calling him *Mr.* Bush when we met in Anaheim on my first day in the league. It's his son who seems to eat only if I've eaten exactly the same dish the previous night. Bush is a great guy, but this particular game he needed a hearing aid.

We were in Oakland when the fairly routine fly goes up toward right-center. I trot over for the catch, hollering all the way. I always call for the ball, of course, but with Bush instead of Bruno playing that game, I called extra loud and long: "I GOT IT! I GOT IT! I GOT IT!"

Bush was hollering, too, but I called him off—"No, I GOT IT." It's my ball because I'm the center fielder. In the noise in Oakland—one of the noisier stadiums, but nothing like our Dome—he didn't hear me. We both arrived at the ball at the same time. Randy caught it right over my head—he's a lot taller—and then we crashed. We really smacked hard but Randy was still standing. I collapsed. His knee had caught mine just inside the kneecap. I laid on the ground, holding my knee. When I saw him throw the ball in, I said, "Way to go, man. You caught it."

He looked down. "Puck, are you all right?"

"No. I'm hurt."

"Aw, man, don't tell me that."

"No, man, I'm hurt!"

"Puck, you gotta get up! My career could be over! You've *got* to get up!"

By now Dick Martin, our trainer, and Tom Kelly were on their way out to the scene of the crime. I knew Randy was really anxious, so maybe I laid it on a bit, rolling around in pain. Mark Davidson, playing left field, had joined the group, and Randy was saying how his career could be over with. Finally I figured I was okay and Dick Martin said so, too, so I got up and Randy and Mark and I ran off the field.

Bush was harping at me all the way to the dugout: "Man, you can't do that to me, Puck. My career was in your hands! You just can't!" (I played a similar trick one day back at Calumet High School. Before some big game I rigged up a fake cast on my right arm and showed up at the field that way, looking very sad.)

The Oakland fans are not only loud; they're also crude, probably the crudest we have in the American League. They can really hose down the opposing players. One fan out in the bleachers in center field was always on my case—not in '87, but several years later, if memory serves me. Of course, you expect a little more from the guys in the bleachers. I got to know this guy's voice, yelling at me night after night after night: "Hey, stop the game! Stop the game! The Twins don't have anybody in center field! . . . Oh, there he is. Kirby, stand up! Get off your knees so we can see you!" Other times: "Kiiirby, you're 0-for-3, did you know that?" I heard all this—nothing new—but didn't pay much attention until one game I decided to break the unwritten rule and turn around and find out what this guy looked like. I was curious. I sauntered back toward the fence so I'd have a better chance of spotting him, and when he started in I turned and found him immediately. I guess he was surprised that, after all these games, I had finally acknowledged his presence. That's what these guys want, after all. He must have weighed four hundred pounds! Took up half the row. He called down to me, "What are you looking at, Kirby?" I gestured with my arms outspread to indicate his size and the fans starting laughing and clapping. This guy laughed and I laughed and we had a good time that evening. But he didn't shut up.

I just missed being voted to the All-Star team that year, but the Twins were in first place in the AL West. That's a combination I'd take every time. I was then named to the squad by John McNamara and AL President Bobby Brown, on the strength of my .340 batting average. But Kent Hrbek had a real good first half, too, and he was left off in favor of Mark McGwire, who was having a big year with the A's and deserved the honor, and Pat Tabler of the Indians, who didn't have the stats Kent had. Gary Gaetti was passed over, too, and a lot of guys thought he deserved it.

Kent, who was on the team in '82, his rookie year, got really mad about being left off in '87 and told the reporters he'd never play again on any other All-Star team. He said it wasn't even an All-Star game because it wasn't an All-Star team. That omission cost Kent good money, while I picked up thirty grand. (How about Roger Clemens? He didn't make the team and lost $200,000 as a result. I'd never heard of a bonus that big.)

Even Andy MacPhail joined Kent in complaining about the All-Star selections, claiming that any team that had led the standings for as long as we had—most of the season—should merit more than one player on the team. Minnesota—passed over again in favor of the big-name clubs from the big cities. That was the beef, and it has been that way ever since I've played in Minnesota. The fans feel their team doesn't get any respect. Some of the ballplayers feel that way—Hrbek, for one. I'm not concerned. I've mentioned that it was nice to get a lot of out-of-town votes when I was voted onto the All-Star team in '86, but this is another one of those issues that I let everyone else get worked up over.

Sometimes people ask if I'd get more endorsement work if I played in New York or Los Angeles. Maybe, but I turn down most offers anyway. I never do autograph shows, for example. In one of my first years in the league I signed a contract to do six shows. After the first one I called Tonya and told her how uncomfortable I had been, taking money from little kids. I had signed a contract so I did the other five shows that year, but that was it. Never again. Other guys do the card shows, and that's fine, but I'm not comfortable with it. With most of the other offers, it comes down to a question of time versus money, and I'm usually more interested in having my time for myself and my family. I do like to do a few things, and I often donate that income to a charity.

Reporters ask if I wish I played in New York or L.A., where I might be a big media star, and my answer is *No!* I make plenty of money, and I know what it's like in the Big Apple. Andy MacPhail said that if I played in New York they'd be building statues to me. But I don't crave publicity. I'm popular enough in Minnesota, nice, clean, calm Minnesota.

I also like nice, clean, calm Milwaukee. I love the place, in fact, because I had the best weekend of my professional life there in August as we were rolling toward the division championship. That weekend brought back memories of the Junior College World Series in Colorado, when I was in another zone. It happened to me again at old County Stadium in Milwaukee, home of the league's best bratwurst. However, this weekend was kicked off with a meal at my sister June's house.

June is a great cook, and my brother-in-law, Tommy, is too, so I always eat with them at least once on every trip through Milwaukee. June picks me up at the hotel and takes me to their house for some home cooking, always my favorite meal: fried chicken and french fries—not the frozen fries, either, but real ones. June fries the chicken, Tommy slices the potatoes and fries them. I'd been enjoying this meal with them since my high school days, when they were still living in Chicago. I'd take some buddies to their place on weekends to eat fried chicken and play cards in the basement. If one of my friends had a car we'd ride, but if not, the chicken was worth the long walk, a mile and a half or so. Sometimes I borrowed June's car. She'd always say no but Tommy would always say yes. He'd usually loan me a few dollars as well. I paid him back every time.

But now we're talking Milwaukee in 1987. On this particular Saturday my pal Al Newman joined me for the usual feast.

Afterward, on the way to the stadium, I made some remark to him about wishing I could hit as well as my sister and brother-in-law could cook. We got to the park early (I'm always early) and the Brewers were taking BP when I walked onto the field. Tony Oliva called me over and said he wanted to talk about hitting. I wasn't surprised. My hitting for a couple of months had been on again, off again. I'd struck out three times in the All-Star game, and that was embarrassing. Maybe I was trying too hard to put that episode behind me. I don't know. I do know I wasn't feeling great at the plate, lunging at the ball, swinging not just at bad pitches, which is my habit, but at *terrible* pitches. Tony and I sat down on the tarp down the left field line and before he said anything, I picked up a bat lying there and waved it around a couple of times and said, "Tony, man, I feel great today. Check me out today. I don't know what it is."

We talked a little about staying with the ball, etc., all the usual stuff, and then it was our time to take batting practice. While we were walking to the batting cage I repeated what I'd said. The bat just felt great in my hands that day. And sure enough, in BP every ball I hit was a bullet. Right field line, left-center, center field! Everywhere—like a shot out of a cannon. I usually rev it up and hit well in BP, but this was even better than usual. I was chattering away, like I often do, challenging TK or whoever was throwing to make me work.

"Give me a challenge!"

"Bring your best!"

"That don't cut it!"

"That's outa here!"

"Hey, don't dare come in here like that!"

Trash talk like that helps me concentrate. I'm not one of these guys like Hrbek, Bush, Chili Davis, who need total silence. Now during the game can be another matter. I don't mind the usual give-and-take chatter with the catcher, because I can hold my own there, but Tony Peña with the Red Sox can drive you crazy.

"Come on, baby, come on!"

"Cover second! I'm throwin'!"

"Watch out down there!"

Constantly yelling something to somebody, hollering at the pitcher, anything. Tony doesn't care, but I wonder how his teammates feel about it. I don't think he's doing it to hassle us—the hitters—but I've turned around sometimes and said, "Tony, please, shut up. *Please.*" Maybe he does.

In Milwaukee, I think B. J. Surhoff and Bill Schroeder, the Brewers' catchers that weekend, could have sung at the top of their voices and held onto my legs and I would have hit the ball hard. I went four-for-five in the Saturday game, two home runs, two singles. That was great but not unheard of. I had seventeen four-hit games in those first three years in the majors, and I'd hit two homers in a game before.

But then came Sunday. Before that game I told Tony Oliva I felt the same as I had Saturday. I could feel I was still in that zone.

Tony said, "That's good! That's good!"

Crack! Crack! Crack! Crack! *Crack!* I was already five-for-five in the game, with another homer, when we came up in the ninth inning. With two outs Greg Gagne swings and misses on the third strike, but the ball rolls to the screen and he beats the throw to first. So I get a break and a chance to come up for the sixth time. But conditions are tough. The shadows from the stands are in the way, and Dan Plesac is on the mound. He was the stopper for the Brewers, and throwing hard fastballs and sliders. Even he remembers what happened next; we talked about it later. He throws a fastball low and away—tough, tough pitch—and I don't know how it happened but I kicked my leg and swung. Boom! Home run to right field like a bullet. Exaggerating, of course, Plesac said people could have been knocked unconscious by that shot. My buddies went wild. We were having a great season anyway, those games in Milwaukee moved us back in front of the Oakland A's in the Western Division, and the guys were happy for me and themselves and everybody. Then another really nice thing happened. The Brewers fans gave me an ovation when I trotted out to the field.

Six-for-six, two homers, two doubles, two singles. Ten-for-eleven for two games, four homers (two to left field, two to right). I hadn't had any homers for a couple of weeks, but the fourteen total bases on Sunday set the single-game record for the Twins, and the ten hits in consecutive nine-inning games set the AL record (Mickey Hatcher had shared the old one, nine hits) and tied Rennie Stennett's modern-day major league record. Every ball I hit that weekend was hard. No getting jammed that weekend. Every time on the meat of the barrel. The one out I made was a line drive to second base.

I've never felt that way since, and if I never do again, that's all right, because I felt that way once. And I also took a grand slam away from Robin Yount in the sixth inning of the game on Sunday. The fence at County Stadium has a cushion, and then above that some chain-link. My glove was over the top of that chain-link. A guy tagged to score on the play, but then we got a double play and won the game. That weekend was just an incredible two days of baseball for me, and I'll never forget them. I'm always careful to give my sister June credit because she started it off with her fried chicken. Now June's friends give her a hard time about feeding me because they're all big

Brewers fans and they don't want me to go six-for-six or ten-for-eleven again.

A couple of thousand fans met the Twins at the airport after that weekend, and they were shouting my name. And this time it wasn't just Tonya's family, either.

On Tuesday, our next game, I had two hits going to my last at-bat, and I didn't know at the time that a third hit would have tied another modern-day major league record of thirteen hits in three games. But no matter—I grounded out to second base. I also broke my bat on that swing, so I had no regrets about shipping it to Cooperstown for an exhibit.

That bat was a C-243, Rod Carew's model. When I first came to the big leagues I used a real light bat, 34 inches, 31 ounces, because I was just a base hit hitter. I didn't know anything about home runs. Then in '86, the year I hit all the homers, I switched to Carew's longer, heavier model—35 inches, 33 ounces. Once again, this was Tony Oliva's idea. Two ounces might not sound like much extra weight, but it's a tremendous difference to a hitter. "You can swing a heavier bat," Tony said. "It's all mental. You can hit with any bat you want." Now I have my own bat model, the P-339, with the same specifications as Carew's bat. The "339" was my average when I won the batting title in '89.

During the course of the season my hands swell up for a variety of reasons and the thin-handled bat might not feel right, so I'll switch to the P-116. Carmen Castillo used that bat, and I hit with it once and started hitting the ball real well. It has a very thick handle, 35 inches, 33 ounces. And sometimes I'll use 32 ounces when I'm not feeling as quick. And sometimes when I'm feeling real, real good I'll use a 35-ounce bat; I also use that during batting practice.

• • •

We sewed up the AL West playing in Texas, with about a week to go. By then we were playing with real confidence, and the strangest thing happened in the big clubhouse celebration after the game. Al Newman, Mark Davidson, and myself already had a club we called The Dawgs. Each of us had two "Dawg" T-shirts, one red and one blue, with "YOU GOTTA BE A DAWG" lettered on the back. Davidson brought in the T-shirts but I had started the whole business sometime earlier in the year because I've always said you gotta be a "dawg" to play this game: play dirty, play hurt, play sick, play when you don't feel like coming to the park, period.

Celebrating the division title in Texas, the Dawgs got on the floor and started barking. We were good pals, and this barking business just happened. I have no explanation. Must have looked pretty strange. Must also have looked pretty fun, too, because Danny Gladden, my mate in left field, started begging to be in our club. He was just dying to be a Dawg. It was pathetic. We told him if he would get down on his knees and crawl around the clubhouse barking . . . we'd *consider* his application. So he did.

The next day Danny comes to the park all excited about becoming an official Dawg at last.

"Oh, man, I'm a Dawg. A Dawg! Where's my T-shirt?"

He was beside himself. Al and Mark and I just looked at each other, shaking our heads. We had to explain to Danny that there'd been some kind of mistake. We had said the previous night that we would *consider* his application. Well, we did that, but it wasn't approved. He didn't have the qualifications. Gladden was crushed. What exactly were the qualifications to be a Dawg? Well, you just had to be a Dawg to know a Dawg. Gladden was really sore he couldn't get in.

The Dawgs kept going strong the next year. When we'd

come to the clubhouse and it seemed like the guys needed some revving up, Mark and Al and I would put on our Dawg shirts and start barking. Danny would start circling the dog pound just begging to be allowed inside, and we'd meow at him. Tom Kelly and some of the players would usually join in at Gladden's expense, wanting to know where his Dawg T-shirt was. How could he be out of *uniform?* Or wasn't he even a *member?!* Oh, that hurt him.

Mark went from the Twins to the Astros, and then he joined Charlie Manuel in Colorado Springs; Al went to the Rangers. We never actually disbanded The Dawgs, and the three members might still greet each other with "How you doin', Dawg?" I still have my blue T-shirt, and wear it. I don't know where the red one is.

Maybe we were The Dawgs in 1987 because the Twins were the underdogs all season, as well as going into the play-offs. Our record of 85-77 was the worst among the four division champions, and only the ninth best in the majors. When this was pointed out in the press for days on end prior to the first playoff game against Detroit, my usual reply was, "Yeah, but we had the best record in the AL West."

There were all kinds of other negatives on our side, according to the experts. We lost five straight to end the season after clinching in Texas. Detroit had a bunch of players returning from the '84 World Series team, and we had exactly two guys with postseason experience—pitcher Bert Blyleven and Don Baylor, who came over in a late-season deal with Boston. Baylor said quite a few years later, when the salaries were soaring but some guys were complaining anyway, that he'd take off his cleats and go home if two guys ever started whining—Kirby Puckett and Robin Yount. Baylor was by then a coach for the Brewers. You could say that the Pucketts and the Younts of baseball learned a lot of their attitude from the Baylors of the game. He's strictly class and helped the Twins that season. Just his presence would help any team. A real professional. Not flashy.

We had a great home record of 56-25 but were terrible on the road at 29-52. Even though the schedule gave us four home games in the playoffs (and the Series), everybody figured we'd have to win at least one game on the road, and they said so over and over and over. It's no wonder that by the time the Series finally started, all we wanted to do was play. We were tired of talking—and listening.

We took Detroit four-out-of-five, and won two games in their little ballpark. A lot of runs scored, and Bruno and Gladden and Gaetti were our big hitters. Gagne and Lombardozzi, too. I didn't have great games, but that didn't keep Mark Davidson from having fun with me. As a rookie that year he was earning the flat rate, so the playoff and Series money would be useful to him. He started seeing green. He wanted me to remember that every winning run meant more money for him. So if I happened to get on base—which wasn't that often, five hits in the five games—he'd grin out from the dugout and rub his fingers together in the universal sign for "money," or he'd draw dollar signs in the air. Al Newman did it, too. It was a Dawg thing. That team was one loose bunch.

The loosest of us all, probably the craziest guy on the team, Bert Blyleven, won two games on the mound, including the clincher. He's crazy, man. One day during one of his seasons with the Twins he crawled under the bench in his uniform to light somebody's shoestrings. Under the bench! Spit, chewing tobacco, sunflower seeds, old gum, sticky Gatorade, more chewing tobacco, more old gum, you name it, it's under there. And he crawled through it just to light somebody's shoestrings. He got up and all this crud was all over his uniform. Gives me chills just to think about what he did. I guess he wasn't pitching that night, but I wouldn't bet on it. I'd never do that, or the business with itching powder in the jockstrap, that kind of stuff. Blyleven is a *prankster*, I'm a jokester. Other than a few episodes like the fake cast in high school, my humor is verbal.

Then there was the episode in 1986 with the beard. Bert had shaved it one year earlier when he came to the Twins from Cleveland, but he grew a new one in '86. The Twins announced they would fine him fifty bucks a day until he cut it, and Bert said he would file a grievance on the matter. He also said he was just trying to change his luck after a run of bad innings. They resolved that dispute and he kept his beard. Nobody ever said anything about my goatee, which I've had since '86 or so. It was a little annoying in '92 when Mark McGwire went to the goatee and got credit for making it a fad among the players. I think I was the first, years before Mark. But that's the way it goes. The big power sluggers get all the glory.

Unfortunately, the visiting clubhouse in Detroit was so small The Dawgs didn't have room to get down and bark during the '87 celebration. But we did have enough room to drink the bubbly. That was the most jammed room I've ever been in, and Andy MacPhail ducked into the training room, trying to get some space. But we found him hiding in there and poured champagne all over him and I gave him a big bear hug and yelled, "Andy, man! Way to go, man! Congratulations! I want a new contract! We all want new contracts!"

That broke 'em up, and Andy laughed along with everybody. I'm sure if it were just up to him he'd have given us all new contracts. I had one coming anyway, and he knew that.

The World Series? We won, just like we would four years later, by winning two at home, losing three on the road, and coming home to win the last two. And I played the same both times, not doing much in the first few games, then coming on strong. In '87 I went four-for-four in Game Six, walked once, scored two runs, got a big hit. Hey, we won, man. That's all I know and that's all that counts.

We were supposed to lose, of course, but we didn't pay any attention to that prediction. However, this time we did need the four home games the schedule gave us. After pounding the Cardinals in the first two games in the Dome, we lost the three in St. Louis, getting a total of eighteen hits in twenty-seven innings. We were hopping mad after that showing. No way this team gets eighteen hits in three games. I was mad, for sure, and took extra batting practice before Game Six. For the most part, the Cards' pitchers had made me look pretty bad chasing their junk. My reputation as a free swinger preceded me to the Series, naturally, and I played right into their strategy of pitching me off the plate, way off the plate, and expecting me to get anxious and swing at anything out there. I fell into that trap, I'll admit it. I was very upset with myself. Before the sixth game I watched some videos of my swings, which I seldom do, and they made real clear how I'd been overanxious time after time.

So the first at-bat against John Tudor in Game Six, I just waited, waited, waited, and drove in Gladden with a single to left. I waited the next at-bats, too, and got more hits. Hrbek hit a grand slam, Don Baylor launched one, everybody hit and we went home that night after stomping them 11-5, and ready to settle things with one last game in 1987. And we won that game, 4-2. It turned out that I was in the middle of the action, for better or worse. Willie McGee made a great catch at the wall in dead center field off me in the third. Whitey Herzog changed pitchers before I came up in the fifth, replacing Joe Magrane, a left-hander, with Danny Cox. I understood Whitey's move because I'm always happy to see a left-hander on the mound, and Cox was a hard-throwing right-hander. And he threw hard on the first pitch to me, but I was ready and hammered a double to right-center to score Greg Gagne. The crowd noise then was off the scale—but it dropped some when I tried to make third base on a pitch in the dirt. Out by a mile.

But we scored an insurance run in the eighth and Jeff Reardon saved the game and the season for Viola and the Twins. A lot of people, including some of the Cards, gave credit to our fans for our wins at home, and I don't disagree. The place was rocking, literally. The noise level was unbelievable; some of the players wore earplugs. It's a good thing our outfield was so used to playing with each other, because communication was impossible once the ball was in the air.

I'll never forget that ninth inning. I had never been as nervous, not even in my first game in the majors three years earlier, and I've never been anywhere near as nervous since then. On our way to our positions in the outfield I told Danny Gladden and Tom Brunansky that I could literally hear my heart beating—even above the crowd noise! For the first and last time in my career I was pleading that the ball *not* be hit to me. I was terrified I'd make the critical mistake. And wouldn't you know it? The first batter lifts a high pop to short center. Not a tough chance but I'm telling myself the whole way— "Please don't miss it! Please don't miss it!" I squeezed that ball with both hands and looked in my glove to make absolutely sure it was in there. What a relief—and then more relief when the next two outs went somewhere else.

I hate to end the story about the World Series on a down note, but the truth is that the victory parade through downtown Minneapolis that year was horrible. A picture on the wall in our den tells it all: I'm sitting in the car in my aviator hat—for protection!—not looking very happy, and Tonya is sitting beside me absolutely terrified. We felt like animals in a cage, surrounded by the whole city, it seemed, some of whom were drunk, of course, and acting like animals themselves. There wasn't nearly enough crowd control. The people stormed the cars. Feet got run over. People were grabbing at me, at Tonya. People yelled, "Grab her coat!" People were throwing rolls of toilet paper, and not so they would unfurl and float down like confetti. They threw them *at* us, hard, from twenty feet. Beer bottles, cans, apples were flying. I got dinged on the head a couple of times. We had to stop twice to empty the car of all the debris.

I was scared to death and Tonya was literally shaking with fear. She ended up on the floor with her arms over her head. It took two hours for the cars to crawl through downtown Minneapolis, and downtown Minneapolis isn't that big. That wasn't a celebration of the first world championship for Minnesota. That was more like a riot, from my point of view. Sometimes standing on the ball field I get the feeling of being in a zoo, on display. That day in Minneapolis I felt like I was trapped in a cage. I haven't visited a zoo since that day, because now I have sympathy for the animals.

The whole episode was just a shame, because the fans at the ball games had been tremendous all year. I don't know who these people on the streets that day were, but I have a hard time believing they were the real fans of the Minnesota Twins. The parade over in St. Paul was a lot better, with barricades keeping everyone back from the cars. And the 1991 victory parade through the Twin Cities was better still, because the players rode in pickups instead of cars, and the police were a lot more aggressive keeping people back.

After that World Series, life was never the same for me in Minnesota. No more quiet meals in restaurants or strolls through shopping malls. Things would get even more ridiculous after the '91 Series, four years later. Two months after that victory I was Christmas shopping in Toys "Я" Us when a woman and her two little kids came up for an autograph. I was busy, I had my hands full, if I started signing autographs in that store, when would it end? When they turned out the lights? I explained this very politely to the lady.

"You're serious?! You mean you're not going to sign this?!"

"No, ma'am, I'm not. I'm not signing anything. I'm Christmas shopping for my family, ma'am."

And she cursed me out! Loudly. Yelling and screaming. Everyone in the store could hear her. Tonya says I shouldn't let people get away with that, but was I supposed to get in a shouting match? The lady finally left, yelling all the way. When I was in the checkout line, other shoppers apologized for that lady and told me that I was right and that I had handled the situation pretty well. Nevertheless, I don't go shopping very much. I have yet to visit the Mall of America.

That winter after the '91 Series people were steadily coming up to my own front door. Now, some of them were kids, and maybe they didn't know better, so I'd politely explain that this was the only place where I enjoyed a private life. When adults came to the door, I was still polite, but not as polite, I admit. I don't sign at my own front door. Sorry. Willie Mays doesn't get my autograph at the front door. This is the only place we have some privacy.

During the season, on the road, you hope to have a little fan-free time in the hotel, but it doesn't always work out that way. New York's pretty good, surprisingly enough. They keep the autograph-seekers from clogging that hotel lobby. In Chicago they can't come in the lobby, either, but there are only two ways in and out, and they've got those covered. They also know when we come and go. They know in Minnesota, too, at the Metrodome, and this past year ('92) I had to switch my routine. I used to park and go in the front door at the Metrodome, but a hundred or more fans started gathering there every day last season. They'd start pushing when I got out of my car and I'd have to say, "Look, no pushing or I'm not going to sign." And you're always going to miss some people, and that's when you get the real jerks. And I don't like signing for the obvious scalpers, but they can always get a little kid to come forward. You can't win in those big-crowd situations, so I just started avoiding them. There's nothing wrong with that, is there?

Halloween at our house is unbelievable. Parents drive up our driveway with their kids, so these aren't our neighbors. One boy told Tonya and me this past year that we hadn't given him and his brothers and sisters enough candy. We gave them plenty of candy. "We want more!" The boy pushed Tonya's arm aside and stepped into the house to get more candy from the jar while his parents sat out in the car laughing.

Nobody owns me. I'm sorry if that sounds harsh, but it's the truth. There have to be some limits. And that goes double for certified mail! I don't answer fan mail I get at home, even the certified stuff I sign for without realizing what it is. (I think someone publishes a book with the addresses of ballplayers and celebrities.) I get presents for me and my family, rosary beads, things that look like voodoo dolls, all kinds of stuff. If it comes to the ballpark, I respond. If it comes to my home, I don't.

For a couple of years Tonya and her family and I took care of all the mail, and it was a fun family project. We had a system for licking the envelopes, addressing them, everything. But following my first All-Star game in 1986, the mail that came to the Metrodome started getting out of hand and then it really shot up after the '87 Series—100, 150 letters a day. I had become more popular, but my autograph on a baseball card had gone way up in value, too. We had to turn the job over to the Twins, and they came up with a good system. Some of the mail can be handled by the office, some comes to my locker, where Clayton Wilson, one of the assistant clubhouse men, helps me sort the different requests. Clayton is invaluable. I can turn phone calls over to him if I'm rushed and he'll take the information and talk to me about it later, or send a signed photograph, or whatever.

The rosary beads are a story in themselves. I put them in my locker and forgot about them until some weeks later when I mentioned them to Tonya in passing.

"How long have you had them?" she asked.

"About a month," I said.

"Isn't that about how long you haven't been hitting so well?"

What could I say? Tonya told me to get to the ballpark and throw the beads away. Maybe some nut had put the hex on them. I did throw them away and got a couple of hits that night, and hit well the rest of the year—1992. I cannot explain it.

· · ·

My name and face started showing up in all kinds of strange places after the '87 World Series. The Twins came out with the Kirby Bear, this cuddly teddy bear, and they sold thousands or gave them away with big ticket purchases. I endorsed a pancake mix—a "great batter"—and I also went on a winter caravan promoting the Twins. Thanks to Dan Gladden I almost lost my life on that junket. We were up in Alexandria, Minnesota, the first stop, and were staying at the Radisson resort there, a gorgeous place right on the lake. In my two winters in Minnesota I'd acquired a taste for snowmobiling, so I set up an early-morning run for Danny and me before we were scheduled to leave for the next stop. We spoke at the banquet the night before, then went out with the folks who set up the event, got a little sleep, and then met at the snowmobiles at 6:30 A.M. The Radisson people were happy to outfit us with suits, gloves, boots, and everything else.

There are two versions of what happened next. My story, and I'll stick to it till the day I die, I don't care what Gladden says, is that I knew how to ride a snowmobile and he didn't. After all, who was living in *Arizona* at the time? But Gladden's version is that he was the pro rider and was just pretending he didn't know anything about it, so I'd have to demonstrate what I knew. My version: Off we go on a golf course, real smooth and covered with fresh snow. I was showing him how everything worked on the machine, and he was all excited. Then I went around this tree and flipped my snowmobile over. Maybe it was the blades or something, I don't know, but I was driving correctly. Danny started teasing me about what I knew about snowmobiles, and I didn't want to hear it. It wasn't a close call, really, but flipping one of those things is still a little scary.

I had another off-season snowmobile episode with the guy who played on the other side of me in the outfield, Tom Brunansky. Tonya and Bruno's wife, Colleen, were good friends and we spent a lot of time together during the winter. One year Bruno got a snowmobile for Christmas and I was given one for doing some promotional work. We took them to Bruno's house on Lake Minnetonka, where we'd venture out on the snow and ice.

They plow a double-lane highway on this lake for ice fishing. Cars drive out there. (But not my car. I hate ice fishing almost as much as I hate golf.) The snowbanks from this plow job get three or four feet high, and Bruno and I got daring one day and decided to see how far we could jump, using one bank as a ramp to jump over the second one. After two or three jumps we decided to really gas it over the first hump, but when I got in the air my sled was a little sideways and I went flying off in one direction while the sled plowed on for hundreds of yards. Bruno said I didn't look too pleased when I finally stood up in the snow. If I got hurt snowmobiling, I don't think the Twins would have to pay me. I know Carney Lansford with the A's got hurt snowmobiling. I haven't done anything like that ramp jumping since that day on the lake.

Another day Bruno and I had been riding around for a couple of hours and decided to go visit Kent Hrbek, who lived on the other side of the lake. Herbie joined us on his four-wheeler and we all drove down to John Butcher's place. Then we all drove onto the lake to look inside Hrbek's icehouse. He has a heater, a TV, a refrigerator. It's cozy in there. Then it started to snow and we said, "Well, we'd better get going before we get snowed in out here." Kent took off for his place while Bruno and I headed for his house. The snow was coming down hard by now. And soon—total whiteout, man, you couldn't see anything. After riding for a while Bruno slowed down on his snowmobile and I pulled up on mine and lifted my visor with a strong questioning look.

"Yeah, what, Puck?" He was defensive.

"Don't tell me we're lost."

"Okay, I won't tell you."

"You don't know where you're at?!"

"I knew until I couldn't see anymore." He laughed. I didn't. I'm a city boy. What do I know about being lost in the snow?

"Look," he went on, "we just follow this shoreline and we'll definitely find the house."

He admitted later he said this just to keep me under control. We drove along and somehow Bruno realized that we had gotten off the main body of the lake. Then he slowed down and I pulled over again and raised my visor and just looked at him. He calls it "that look." You know, that look when you're not too happy with someone. But he said he had finally recognized a house. "I know where we're at," he claimed, and it turned out this time he was right. Bruno still laughs at how fast I rode off that lake when I saw his house. "Why not?!" I say. I didn't want to give him any more chances to screw up.

More than just snowmobiling and signing autographs in restaurants was going on that winter. I also had my contract negotiation. At long last I was eligible for arbitration, so I had some leverage this time. And Ron Shapiro and I intended to use it because even Andy MacPhail had said the previous year that I was deferring some income in 1987. I wanted to get what everybody else with my stats was getting. I'd finished the year hitting .332, with twenty-eight homers, thirty-two doubles, five triples—almost one in every three hits for extra bases. I was third in the MVP voting behind George Bell and Alan Trammell. I was an All-Star. And the Twins had won the World Championship, don't forget.

That was the year after Andre Dawson had given the Cubs a signed blank contract and asked management to fill in the amount they would pay him. That's how badly Andre wanted to play in the National League and on a grass field. And he had a great year. At the end of the season he still refused to get confrontational with the Cubs, even though they had gotten the deal of the century in '87. He did, however, want them to be fair.

I shared Andre's attitude about not wanting or needing a lot of front-page confrontation, and I, too, wanted my organization, the Twins, to be fair. I was thinking arbitration would be necessary. I'm not a confrontational kind of guy, and I'd heard about arbitration from some of the other players, especially Phil Bradley, an old friend who had a bad experience with arbitration in Seattle. But Ron Shapiro had had good experiences with arbitration with some of his other clients, and he convinced me that we could do it without a negative impact on my relationship with the Twins.

When you go to arbitration, the player submits a figure and the club submits one. The arbitrator picks one or the other, nothing in between. We wanted to propose a number that was sufficiently realistic on the low side that it might win the arbitration, yet was high enough to get the Twins to negotiate a settlement, if possible. We came up with $1.35 million. The Twins were offering $930,000.

Ron's brief was as big as a dictionary. He and Michael Maas and others in the office in Baltimore spent hundreds of hours getting their numbers together and preparing an oral argument to make to the arbitrator. And Ron continued to talk with Andy MacPhail to reach a settlement. For this and all the other contract negotiations I've had with the Twins, I'm in close touch with Ron but I'm not in on every single fluctuation. I don't want to overfocus on this stuff. I'm playing baseball whatever I'm paid. It's Ron's job to get me the best deal he can, and his team does a great job. I have total faith in them.

But nothing much really happened before the scheduled day in Chicago in February. We were all supposed to gather at an airport hotel, and it was snowing and people had a hard time flying in. Tonya dropped me at the airport in Minneapolis about noon the day before the arbitration, but I didn't make it to Chicago until almost midnight. I joined Ron and Mike for a very late dinner and final consultation.

At 9:00 A.M. all the parties arrived at the meeting room. On one side of the table were Andy MacPhail, the people from the Player Relations department in the commissioner's office, and Tal Smith, former general manager in Houston, now a consultant for the owners. Smith was going to argue the case for the Twins. In fact, Andy MacPhail didn't even need to be there.

On the opposite side of the table were myself, Ron Shapiro, Michael Maas, Mark Belanger from the Players Association, and one or two others. The arbitrator was down at the end of the table. Coffee and juice and muffins were served, and we were just about to get down to business when Andy McPhail looked across the table at Ron and asked, "Can we take a walk?"

They were gone for about forty-five minutes. Mike Maas was with them. The rest of us chatted about the weather.

Then Ron came back and asked me to join them in the lobby, and we sat down and discussed a tentative figure for a one-year deal. What did I think? I thought it was a good figure and said right then, "Let's settle." That deal was for $1,090,000, plus a bonus package that turned out to be worth $120,000.

I had a question: "Who's paying all the expenses for the arbitration meeting?" There were a lot of plane flights involved. I was just curious, and a little naive. I thought maybe the loser in the arbitration had to pay! It turns out that the costs are split between the two sides.

Last-minute agreements like mine before arbitration are not unheard of. One reason it happened in Chicago was that the two numbers were far enough apart that somebody would be a big winner and somebody a big loser. And I'm not sure the Twins wanted to risk tampering with my mental state if they won. As I understood the process, I would have sat at the table and listened to management try to value my production as low as possible. I know Andy MacPhail, and I know he wouldn't want to do that. How could it possibly *help* the relationship between a player and management? It couldn't. Also, I was one of the first of the new class of three-year players in arbitration, so I was going before an arbitrator who had no standard or precedent by which to rule.

That contract made me the sixth Twin with a salary above one million dollars. The others were Viola, Hrbek, Gaetti, Blyleven, and Brunansky. And Jeff Reardon was just a little under that. I was officially a millionaire from that moment on. I didn't take home anywhere near a million dollars, but that didn't matter. I was a millionaire. People ask if a million dollars—or five or ten million dollars—changes your life. It doesn't, really. Of course, there are the "old friends" who come up and introduce themselves after ten years' absence!

Maybe I *kind of* recognize them, but if they were such good friends I'd be sure, wouldn't I? They're after something. But otherwise a million dollars is a million dollars, that's all. You're the same guy. I think I am, anyway. I'm playing ball, regardless of what I'm paid. And as Ron says, my worst-case scenario is still a great scenario. Or as I say to him, "Hey, Big Shooter"—my nickname for Ron—"I'm just an hour's plane flight or a seven-hour car ride from where I came."

S o you won last year. What can you do for us this year? That's always the question in baseball. Would the Twins repeat as World Champions in 1988? Had we been a fluke in '87? Well, we didn't know whether we would repeat, but we knew we could repeat, and we knew we weren't flukes. You don't lead the league in hitting at .261 and call it a fluke. That kind of stuff is really insulting. We could hit, and we knew it. However, I wouldn't necessarily argue that we were the most talented baseball team in 1987 or '88. Talented on paper, that is, with great individual stats, media superstars, and all the rest. The Twins have never been that kind of team as long as I've been with them, and I doubt that they will be as long as Andy MacPhail and Tom Kelly are in charge.

It was in this period—'87, '88, '89—that the Twins became known around baseball as a blue-collar, work-ethic, fundamentally sound, always hustling baseball team. I mentioned that when I described how Tom Kelly took over as our manager. That's the kind of guy TK is, and that's the kind of team he and Andy have molded. TK expects us to give 100 percent and says if we can look ourselves in the mirror and say that we did so, physically and mentally, then he's satisfied.

We're only going to be out on the field three or four hours—whatever it takes to play this game. We're going to hustle, we're not going to embarrass ourselves. While we're here, we might as well play hard. Otherwise, stay at home. Every time we step on the field, we think we'll win the ball game. I don't think any other team in baseball can tell you that. Against Nolan Ryan, Roger Clemens, Dennis Eckersley—it doesn't matter. We believe we'll win.

When somebody screws up, we admit it immediately. Usually, the guy who screwed up is the first one to say so when he gets back to the dugout. We're self-policing. And if somebody doesn't own up, instead of mentioning names one of us might say, "Guys, we don't all have our oars in the water." It's not necessary to mention names. We all saw what just happened on the field—missed cutoff throw, poor communication in the outfield, baserunning screwup.

We like the rowboat story: We all have to row together to make this ball team work. When the Twins step on the field, we're all equal. I feel that way. We feel that way. I might have the biggest salary on the team (now; for years I didn't) and I might get the most press, but my teammates know me, and I don't think I'm better than anyone else. We all have a role to play and a job to do. When a rookie shows up, there's no bull about making him pay his dues, etc. We don't have any initiation stuff like the rookie carrying the bags for veterans. He is welcomed immediately. At the same time, I urge rookies to keep a fairly low profile until they've done something on the field. Don't pop off until you can back it up with performance.

Seldom does Kelly have to do our disciplinary work, but he can and will if necessary, benching major leaguers just like he did when coaching in the minors. Chuck Knoblauch won the Rookie of the Year Award in 1991, but his work ethic slipped a bit at some point, as he'll be the first to acknowledge. Chuck's the ultimate TK-type player: solid fundamentals, a go-getter, and there's no doubt that his rookie season is one of the big reasons we won it all in '91. But one afternoon he found himself scratched from the lineup for a game he expected to start. TK didn't say a thing to him. While on the bench that night "Knob" asked Al Newman if he knew why he had been benched.

Al said, "Chuck, remember that ball you didn't back up?"

"Yeah."

"That's it. Effort, Chuck. Patrol yourself."

We don't have a lot of team meetings because if everyone is always on patrol, there's no need for meetings. If we have something to talk about, we do it informally. If we lose, nobody has to put on a game face. Brian Harper, who has been on a lot of teams, said that one of the great things about playing for Tom Kelly and the Twins is that you don't have to mope around for fifteen minutes after a loss just to show everyone how much it hurts. We have had players who really get angry after losses. Pitchers, for obvious reasons, have that tendency. John Smiley, who came over from Pittsburgh in '92 before leaving for the Reds, would be in a daze for an hour after a bad outing. He once blasted reporters who had the nerve to approach him during that period. Well, that's okay because "Smiles" just hates to lose when he's on the mound. Frank Viola was the same way with the Twins. He joined the club in 1982 after barely a year in the minors, and he got pounded a lot in his first few years, before I arrived, and every loss just tore him up, from what I hear. Frankie just *hated* to lose.

I hate to lose, too, but I could never react like that. I get mad, but I don't think I could stay that mad for fifteen minutes. Then again, I'm not a pitcher. Without a doubt, the angriest I've ever been on a baseball field was early this past year, 1992, in Milwaukee. Shane Mack was having a good series when their pitcher Mike Fetters hit him on the head with a pitch. Shane knows the guy, which makes you think he didn't do it on purpose. Chili Davis knows him, too. I say Fetters threw at Shane on purpose. Anytime I see someone hit on the head, I think it's on purpose. (But I don't know why, because I got hit on the head by Ron Guidry, and I know it was an accident. That was back in the early years when I was leading off for the Twins, leaning out over the plate to stroke a single to right field. Guidry threw a couple of sliders down and in, and I didn't swing at them. I was pretty certain he'd go outside with the next pitch, so I was leaning out looking for it, but Louisiana Lightnin' surprised me with a fastball that ran in on me. Caught me on the earflap. Rang my bell. Guys came running out. Somebody held up some fingers on one hand and asked me, "How many?" I saw eight of them but figured that couldn't be right. "Four," I said, and went on down to first.)

But I thought Fetters had thrown at Shane's head in Milwaukee, and I screamed at him for I don't know how long. "Throw at Puckett, why don't you! You want to hit somebody, hit me!" I lost it that day, I really did. I went berserk. I think I shocked my teammates. I've never been mad like that after a loss.

The Twins don't go around blaming any one player for a loss. There's none of that grumbling on the Twins—second-guessing other players or the manager. I can't remember when I've heard a Twins player second-guess Tom Kelly, even in the confines of a hotel room. You can bet that's not the case on most teams.

Have you noticed the Twins don't sit in the sunshine at the end of the dugout styling in our sunglasses? Nothing against sunglasses, I wear them myself sometimes, it's just not the Twins' way. We're not flashy dudes. With the exception of Shane Mack, we don't even wear high-top shoes. Shane has ankle problems and feels more comfortable in the big shoes. I automatically fit right in with this team—not a high-dollar-type guy. The guys on other teams who are, fine, unless they bring it into the Twins' clubhouse. One day last year a super-star, or almost a superstar, *soon to be* a superstar on another team, strode into our place and started glad-handing his way around the clubhouse. I just sat there. I don't like that stuff. I'd never, never, go to the opposing clubhouse. Say hello to my friend on the field before the game. Meet him outside the park after the game. But go over to his clubhouse and act loud? No way.

If I hit a homer, I don't jog around the bases real slow. I run around fast. I'm not out there to make someone look bad. I don't Cadillac. In real life, I drive a truck. Nobody sat me down as a kid and lectured me about playing this way. It's just the way I've always thought the game should be played. When you're flashy, you're setting yourself up. You might also be hurting the team. I've never seen hard-nosed, basic baseball hurt the team. Never. How could it?

It really bothers me to see an opposing player semirun to first base on a grounder. You cannot take anything for granted. Against Chicago this past year we were down 7-6 in the seventh inning, two outs, nobody on. I hit a grounder to Robin Ventura to third base, whose throw to Frank Thomas was up the line. I sped past Thomas when he tried to slap me with the tag. E-5. Chili Davis followed with a double to score me and tie the game, and we went on to win. If I'm just trotting to first, we lose that game. That kind of play doesn't happen often, but it happens. It shouldn't even be necessary to mention running hard to first base, but not everyone does it. We do on the Twins, but I'm talking about other teams. TK often refers to solid, fundamental baseball as "Field 5," in honor of the field at the new training camp where pitchers and infielders work on basic plays.

I'm so old-fashioned I even use two hands to catch a routine fly ball—although I admit I've been getting away from that lately. You'd be amazed how many compliments I've received from opposing players, opposing coaches, just people who know about baseball—all for catching with two hands. My favorite ballplayers are some of the other two-handers, the guys who just get the job done, thank you. Without knocking anybody else, these are the kind of guys I like to watch play, the guys who remind me of myself: Robin Ventura of the White Sox, Paul Molitor, now with the Jays, Robin Yount of the Brewers, Dave Winfield, now with the Twins, Cal Ripken, Jr., of the Orioles, Eddie Murray of the Mets, Joe Carter of the Blue Jays. If these players couldn't give 100 percent, they wouldn't play. They may not be rah-rah types, but they're *playing*, believe me.

I also consider myself kind of a throwback player. I've been wearing low socks for a couple of years. I picked that up from our pitcher Scott Erickson. I tried the socks that way one game and got four hits, as I recall. Hey, the socks work! I've worn 'em high, medium, now low. I like that throwback look. I think Delino DeShields with Montreal started this trend as a tribute to the Negro League players. That was their style.

Generally speaking, the Twins are not a brawling team. Late in the season last year we almost got into a brawl with Toronto after Scott Erickson hit one of their batters with a pitch. Todd Stottlemyre, one of the Blue Jays pitchers, started yelling from their bench. We started yelling back. The jawing went back and forth when, suddenly, Stottlemyre charged out of their dugout. When that happens, everyone has to follow, and we have to meet the challenge, of course. But the fight never got going. We all just stood around jawing.

There won't be many articles in the papers about the Twins and their DWIs or their fights in bars. In my time with them, about the only fight I remember was the famous one between Danny Gladden and Steve Lombardozzi in 1987. That made news all over the country when the two of them showed up the next day at the ballpark with cuts and bruises, but I never got the full story. It wasn't my business. The fight had been at Gladden's house. Lombardozzi was unhappy in general that season. TK had pinch-hit for him a couple of times and he got mad. Somehow Gladden got involved. On other teams, this stuff happens all the time. With the Twins, that's a major story.

Ask anyone in baseball about the Twins' style or the "Twins mystique," as it's sometimes called around town, and they'll back me right down the line. I'm not trying to build up the Twins as this team that nobody else can be like, but I am emphasizing that when you're talking about the Twins you *are* talking about a *team*. It doesn't take any player long to know that all TK wants is for him to be the best ballplayer he can possibly be. And if Tom Kelly gets a player on the team whom he doesn't believe wants to get to that goal, that guy's history as a Twin. I honestly believe Tom would rather lose with twenty-five hardworking average major league players than win with twenty-five prima donnas. But ask him to be sure about that. He might say that you can't win anyway with twenty-five prima donnas. That's probably right.

A couple of guys who have played recently for the Twins didn't fit in, and to everybody's surprise. Right at the start of the '88 season my pal Tom Brunansky was traded to St. Louis for Tommy Herr. Herr had the reputation of being a ballplayer's ballplayer, a down-in-the-dirt guy, a TK type. That trade should have been one such player for another, just swapping an outfielder for an infielder. But Tommy just never fit in with us. Maybe he didn't like the American League. I don't doubt that switching leagues can be tough for a veteran hitter—learning new pitchers and umpires. In any event, to our eyes he just didn't play Twins-ball, and he was traded back to the National League—Philadelphia—at the end of the season.

Almost immediately we got Wally Backman from the Mets—another National League infielder with the reputation of being a lot more comfortable in a dirty uniform than in a clean one. But Wally wasn't with the Twins long, either. I don't think either of those guys would disagree with the statement that, for whatever reason, they and the Twins just didn't mesh. I can say that without putting the rap on them. I almost never put the rap on another ballplayer because I don't know what's going on with him. Everybody has to go through life as he or she sees fit, and then live with the consequences.

With Herr and Backman, it's easy to see why management thought those two guys would fit right in. When they didn't, they were traded. A real key to our success has been getting people from other organizations who weren't playing to their potential, for whatever reason, but who would fit in and thrive with the Twins. Shane Mack. Chili Davis. Brian Harper.

Having said all this, I have to point to the Oakland A's as a successful team that has a reputation just about the opposite of the Twins'. They're always portrayed as flashy, brawling, bickering in public, criticizing each other all the time, always controversial. Even their manager takes part. After the big Jose Canseco trade last year, La Russa wouldn't even refer to Jose by name. In interviews, La Russa called Jose "the other guy." But the A's also won three American League championships in recent years. The New York Mets were similar back when they were good, and they were good anyway. And the Yankees back in Reggie's era? Always controversial, but they won.

The fact that the Twins were the World Champions in 1987 helped establish this chemistry. No doubt about that. Plus we had won the league, the playoffs, and then the Series despite all the predictions, and all those underdog victories brought us together. A big factor was the way TK used all the players, a policy that Ray Miller had started during his brief tenure as Twins manager. I don't know for sure, but I imagine every player got in a game at least once a week. All of us saw some kind of action, and we all knew our roles.

The following year, however, was a different story. We won ninety-one games in 1988, six more than we won in '87, but the A's stomped the league with 104 victories. Maybe the very first game was an omen. I was tied up watching the NCAA basketball championship, as I remember, and just didn't get around to shaving my head. Then I got my glove on a ball above the wall, but couldn't hold on. That was a three-run homer for Mike Pagliarulo (who joined the Twins in 1991), and we lost to the Yankees 8-0.

I liked Hrbek's line to the press after Opening Day—"You can't count us out yet"—but the season turned out to belong to Oakland. The A's handled us, too, winning eight of the thirteen games. But they didn't intimidate us. Most teams go into Oakland most years and expect to lose. Not the Twins. We know when we play Oakland we're playing one of the great teams, but we don't care about that. They know they can't intimidate the Twins. Just because they have—or had— Canseco and the Hendersons, McGwire, Baines, Eckersley, don't stop thinking it's going to be a tough series against the Minnesota Twins. Sure, they've had a roster full of big-name superstars. Natural ability? They have a lot of natural ability. Those are guys who have been around and can get the job done, you know. But we come to play, and they know it. The A's are a good team, and so are the Twins. They respect us and we respect them. If you look at our record against the A's since 1984, we're ahead 62-55. Case closed.

One of our best games against Oakland was in 1991, on our second trip to the West Coast, when they led us 5-0 after five solo homers—three by Dave Henderson, one each by McGwire and Canseco. In the eighth inning, I knocked in two runners with a single and then Chili Davis drove home two guys, including me, with another single and I just had this *feeling* when I crossed the plate to bring us within a run, down only 5-4. "Here we come!" I shouted. Then Brian Harper hit a three-run blast. Final score: 8-6 Twins. Six solo homers (Harold Baines added one in the eighth) down the drain for Oakland.

People outside the Midwest assume the Twins' biggest

rivalry must be with Oakland, but that's wrong. As far as rivalries and good hard baseball go—that's Milwaukee for the Twins. We go to Milwaukee and seem to have as many fans as they do, and they come to the Metrodome and seem to have as many fans as we do. That's a great rivalry, the Brewers.

That year, 1988, was my hottest ever as a hitter. Twenty-four homers, 121 RBIs. My .356 average was the highest by a right-handed hitter in the American League since Joe DiMaggio's .357 in 1941 (the year Ted Williams hit .406 from the left side). I got an unusual bonus because of that average. Before the season I played in the charity softball game held each February to benefit the battle against sickle-cell anemia. NBC carries the game every year and Bob Costas and I had become friends over the years. In February '88, Bob's wife, Randy, was pregnant and I asked Bob what he and Randy were going to name their baby. Bob said, "I'll tell you what. If you hit .350 this year, we'll name our child Kirby." And if it was a boy, I suppose. Bob must have thought my hitting .350 was a long shot because, as it turned out, he had also promised to name the baby after Randy's brother Keith.

Surprise! Bob and Randy's son is now named Keith Michael Kirby Costas. I like that. Tonya and I might get together with Bob and Randy for dinner during the season, if we can, and this past year Bob was one of the players in my invitational pool tournament—a fair performer with the cue; definitely not a shark.

I was also proud in 1988 to become only the fourth player ever to have 1,000 hits in his first five years in the majors. And the three others who'd done it were old-timers: Joe Medwick, Paul Waner, and Earle Combs. The night in September I joined those three all-time greats, I told the press that I was a hard worker and if you work hard, good things happen. Another one of those famous Puckett clichés that happen to be true. And that year I joined Rod Carew as the only Twin to hit .300, have 200 hits, score 100 runs, and drive in 100 in the same season. The simple truth is I was just *on* the whole year. You throw it and I'd hit it. But I still didn't win the batting title. Wade Boggs hit an awesome .366, and when that happens, you just tip your cap and wait till next year.

Next year, last year, this year—my basic thinking about hitting never changes. I can explain it pretty quickly, too. First, I figure if a pitch is close enough for the ump to call a strike, it must be close enough for me to swing. In other words, I don't worry much about whether it's down the middle or on the corner. Sometimes I've told the guys on the bench, "Okay, okay, I'm going to take a pitch. Believe it or not, I'm going to take a pitch!" Well, I usually couldn't make myself do it, but if I did take the pitch, sure enough, inevitably it's right down the middle. And I know for sure I'll never see that pitch again. So I don't put my destiny in someone else's hands—the umpire's or the pitcher's. I learned that from Tony Oliva, too. I want to control my own destiny. If I swing and miss, I can deal with that. I can sleep at night. But if I think it's a ball and take the pitch and the ump thinks it's a strike, it *is* a strike. I don't want to have to depend on anyone else, so I just swing the bat. When in doubt, swing. Therefore I don't get the strike zone from the umps that some guys get, because it's true that if you have the reputation of having a good eye and being a selective hitter, you tend to get the calls. (It's also true that if you're a pitcher with a justified reputation for having great control, you get the calls. Dennis Eckersley is an example.)

I hear all the talk about this ump's strike zone versus somebody else's, the American League zone versus the National League zone. I don't know or really care. The umps are doing the best they can. But I will say this: Steve Palermo was the best on balls and strikes. If he called you out on strikes, you were legitimately out on strikes.

I very seldom hassle the umps. I learned my lesson from Davey Phillips. When we were in Cleveland for a three-game series my rookie year, Phillips called me out on a bang-bang play at first base. This was when I could really run, and I used to be safe on those plays all the time. (At least I thought I was.) And Davey called me out! I was yelling, "No! No!" and some other words. The following day Davey was calling the balls and strikes behind the plate. Every close pitch was a strike against me. I'm saying a few nouns and adjectives, I'll admit it. The next day Davey's at third base, and I score a run and trot out to center field and he signals me to come over to his position, so I do. And he yelled at me like I'd never been yelled at before. Our noses were touching. "You rookie SOB ?%#!?!!%! You raw rookie telling me about balls and strikes! $%@%#'#!" He followed me all the way from third base to short center field. Since then I've very seldom had any problem with umpires. I don't say anything. I don't see the percentages in arguing. The funny thing about the guys who do argue with the umps about close pitches is that they also take strikes right down the middle. From my position in center field, I have a good view. These guys will take good pitches to hit, then complain about close pitches! That's crazy. I don't have a lot of sympathy, I'll admit.

Early in 1991 I had an occasion to pass on my Davey Phillips experience to our phenom rookie, Chuck Knoblauch.

We were out in Seattle. Chuck had struck out twice, I believe, the last time on a checked swing, and I could tell he was really mad at the ump about some calls. He didn't yell at him, but he was mad. I went over and told Chuck he couldn't afford to let the umpires get to him, and he definitely couldn't afford to get on their bad side.

Don't let the umps or pitchers control my at-bat. That has always been my thinking, but back in 1986 our manager Ray Miller worked with me on taking more pitches. It just didn't fit because, in my mind, that means the umps are controlling the at-bat. But in 1990 I told the guys before the season, on my own, that I was going to get fifty walks. That isn't a lot for most guys, but I'd never had more than forty-one. But I thought for some reason that maybe I could help the team if I got on base a little more often, with walks if necessary. Whatever my thinking was, it was bad. I got those extra walks—fifty-seven, to be exact—but my batting average fell below .300 for the first time in five years, down to .298, and I didn't help the Twins at all because we had a terrible season. Never again.

Wade Boggs can hit and walk, but walking ruins me. When I saw Wade in spring training in 1989, after he'd beat me out for the batting title the previous season, he came up and shook my hand and said, "I just want to tell you, you're awesome. Hitting like that *and you don't walk.*" I appreciated that coming from Wade because he can really hit. And walk.

Wade and I talk about hitting all the time. It comes down to this: He can't believe the way I hit, and I can't believe the way he hits. I'm so spontaneous and he's so mechanical. He takes pitches right down the middle! Thinks nothing of it! I could never be like Wade, get up there and take, take, take. No way. I wouldn't be making this living if I played that way!

Of course, Wade couldn't make a living going up there like me, hack, hack, hack. He's looking for the certain pitch in a certain area that he wants to do a certain thing with. Me, I don't care what I do with it, right field, left field, high, low, I just want to put my bat on the ball and maybe something good will happen. That's the truth. Anybody will tell you. That's the way the Puck hits. I try never to worry about my average. I think about hits. If I get the hits the average will come.

My strength and power come mainly from quick, strong wrists. The high leg kick and shift of weight give me what home run power I have, but more basic are the strong wrists. That's totally different from, say, Mark McGwire. He swings more with his body and legs and uppercuts the ball. I swing down on the ball. I get my homers when the pitchers get one up and I hit the line drive out. I don't remember ever hitting one of those towering shots like McGwire and Strawberry and Canseco. I repeat, I am not a "home run hitter" like those guys.

I'm a first ball hitter because that's often the best pitch to hit. The pitcher's always trying to get ahead of you. But after all these years, the pitchers know I'm looking for that first one, too, and they're more careful. With two strikes on me—a situation I try to avoid—I choke up a little, but I'm still as aggressive as ever. If I lose that, I'm no good.

The problem is that pitchers try to get me out without throwing strikes. I know that. We had a game last year against Boston in which Danny Darwin struck me out twice and threw only one strike. But the third time up I changed my style completely. He had a no-hitter going, and I wanted to get a solid hit—nothing cheap—and break it up. (But if it had to be cheap, I'd take that, too!) I spread my stance really wide and did not stride at all. No leg kick. I call this my "Paul Molitor swing." Just put the bat on the shoulder and wait for the ball, instead of getting all fired up and kicking my leg and everything. I'll use that no-stride swing in BP sometimes to make myself slow down, and I'll use it occasionally in games when I'm overanxious and therefore way out in front of everything. This time I just used my hands and knocked a single to center. Darwin scuffed the mound with his shoe.

I like aggressive pitchers. Come at me and I'll come at you. Clemens, Morris, Juan Guzman. Ain't no nibblin'. Here we go. Some people believe you'll get one good pitch to hit in every at-bat. But I don't agree. Look at Rick Sutcliffe. He never gives in to the batter. Forget it. You will not see the pitch down the middle. He throws what's best for him. There are a lot of pitchers like that. Frank Tanana's the same way. Frankie Viola, my good buddy, he'll throw that circle change-up or whatever it is on 3-1. Now, with Nolan or Roger, you know what's coming.

I don't play cat and mouse with the pitchers. Lefties, righties, I'm hackin'. The same old Puck. Throw it, I'm swingin'. When in doubt, swing. Somebody asked me one time about my philosophy playing center field. My *philosophy*, huh? I paused for a few moments and replied, "Catch everything." The same goes for batting: "Hit everything."

I don't go up there guessing, either. Oh, no, man. Every time I guess I mess up, although that's how most guys make their living. I don't *try* not to guess. I just don't. I go up there and look for the ball. Of course, I'm always thinking the pitcher will throw a hanging breaking ball—I'm ready for that—because those are the pitches you can't miss. You can't afford to miss a hanging curve or a change-up or fastball right down the middle. You can't afford to be caught looking at those. You have to take advantage of those (unless you're Wade Boggs).

But I do go up there to get jammed! I don't care if a pitcher jams me. Just like Robin Yount, Paul Molitor. They go up to get jammed, too. Ask 'em. Maybe this sounds strange to a lot of Little League coaches, so let me explain.

When you get jammed, you don't hit the inside pitch on the meat of the bat, but down on the trademark. However, you can still hit that pitch hard. I have an inside-out swing, and I can hit that inside pitch hard to right field. Knowing that you can hit the pitch even if you're jammed gives you the confidence to keep your front shoulder in and not bail out. If the ball's on the outside part of the plate, beautiful, it's all yours. If it comes inside, you'll be jammed, sure, but you can still hit the ball hard. You can. You're not going to hit a homer when you're jammed, but you can hit a hard single, and meanwhile you've got the outside part of the plate protected. You only get jammed on fastballs, of course. Bring that hanging curveball inside and I'm going to pull that ball.

When Shane Mack came over to the Twins from San Diego, he was always worried about getting jammed. I told him, "Good hitters *get jammed*." He had heard this theory, of course, but we worked hard to convince Shane. It's mainly a mental thing.

The alternative to having a positive attitude about being jammed is to go up believing that you can have *either* the inside or the outside half of the plate covered, but not both. This is negative and dangerous. Hitters who use the whole field should learn to accept being jammed and also be ready to pull the ball with power when the opportunity arises. By the way, I got jammed on the pitch I hit to break up Danny Darwin's no-hitter.

I'm not particularly interested in knowing what pitch is coming. I don't want to know, I don't care. Problems start when you *think* you know what's coming. Maybe the catcher is messing with you and says, "Hey, man, here comes the curveball." Some hitters might say back, "Hey, man, don't say that." Others might think, "Okay, it is a curve." Some will believe the catcher, some think he's lying, other guys get caught in the middle and don't know. It messes with their minds. I don't care. Tony Peña can say anything he wants. I say, "Okay, let me see it!"

There are a couple of guys on the mound who are tougher on me than the others, but I'm not going to give them the pleasure of telling them who they are! But the truth is, these pitchers are ones you might be surprised about. They're not necessarily the big-name throwers. Nor am I going to reveal the pitchers I can't wait to hear called into the game. But they know who they are.

Against a knuckleballer like Charlie Hough I move way up in the batter's box. Try to hit the pitch before it moves too much. I'm also right on top of the plate against these guys. Joe Niekro taught me that trick when he was with the Twins in '87. "Puck," he said, "the thing a knuckleballer doesn't want to see—his worst nightmare—is the guy right on the plate because then he doesn't know where to start the knuckleball off." But this strategy hasn't worked so far for me. Haven't done all that much damage off Hough! But, hey, it's better than just going up there without a plan. I also move up on guys who throw slow.

Another key to hitting is to *keep hitting*. If you get one or two hits early in the game and it's a blowout either way, you've got to keep your concentration on the third and fourth and fifth at-bats, even though they probably don't mean that much in the game. Sure, I get paid a lot to do what I do, but, money or no money, the fire has to be there in the first inning and in the ninth inning. And it is for most major leaguers or they never would have made it this far. I'm not sure the fans understand this. We're competitive. It's in our blood. We want more hits off the pitcher! We want to win.

I have my slumps but, usually, I know what I'm doing wrong. After all, I've been in the big leagues nine years! I'd better know by now. If I'm hitting the ball off the end of the bat, that can only mean one thing. My front shoulder is flying out and I'm pulling off the ball. If I'm just in a rut in general, I'm probably swinging at too many bad pitches. I get too aggressive, swing at anything, the pitchers and catchers see this, and then I'll get nothing decent the rest of the night, or the series, nothing at all until I settle down. That's what happened in the '87 World Series against the Cardinals, as I explained. Only when I started to be patient in Game Six did I have any success. You can be a successful free swinger, but you have to be smart, too.

I might watch a video if I'm not doing too well, but not often. I'll go in and our hitting coach, Terry Crowley, will run a series of swings and say, "See, Puck, there's your shoulder pulling out." It can help when you see it, but I'm not a video buff like some guys.

I have never tried switch-hitting. Never. Never. Insanity. It's hard enough to get hits just from one side of the plate.

Pinch-hitting? I'm the worst. In fact, I drive 'em crazy when I'm on the bench. Just too antsy. Don't know what to do. Al Newman used to tell me to get on down the bench, down all the way to the end, where people couldn't hear me.

"Maybe this day off is helping your muscles," he'd say, "But it's driving your mind crazy, and ours, too." It's true, I just can't sit still or keep my mouth shut. I go through a lot of sunflower seeds and chewing gum.

But DH'ing is fun! I did it quite a bit in '92, and I hit well. It's not like a day off. I still feel like I'm in the game. My legs get a rest. I get to concentrate on hitting. I've talked to Dave Winfield about the DH. He likes it, and I might like it sometime in the future, too. The odd thing about the DH role is when I'm watching from the bench while the Twins are in the field, I forget where I am. If the ball is hit toward center, I react: "I've got it!" or "I may not have it!" Then I remember I'm standing in the dugout.

Before the '88 season I played a lot of basketball for conditioning and went on a diet without red meat for a couple of weeks, and lost ten pounds. Ever since, I've eaten very few steaks. After that season, traveling in Japan with an All-Star contingent from the United States playing one of their All-Star teams, I changed my diet again. The media from America had a party for the players and one of the tables was loaded with iced-down oysters. Fresh, big ones. Vince Coleman and Willie McGee and all these guys are oyster lovers and were trying to get me to taste one. I told them, "I don't eat those slimy things." And I meant it. But they kept teasing me and finally I tried one—and loved it. I couldn't believe it. Douse 'em with some cocktail sauce, lemon, and a little Tabasco and I'd rather have oysters than just about anything. I can easily handle a couple of dozen.

Our team that year in Japan included Fred McGriff,

Harold Reynolds, Paul Molitor, Barry Larkin, Alan Trammell, Bobby Bonilla, and a bunch of other great players—and Willie McGee and Vince Coleman, of course. Sparky Anderson was the manager. Our wives were invited also and they probably saw more of Japan than we did. We didn't have time to do much but play baseball, based in Tokyo with several two- and three-day road trips. We traveled by bus a lot, but we also took the bullet train. Really fast, really clean. I mean immaculate. Not a speck of dirt on it—a lot different from the El in Chicago I used to ride on.

I became a popular attraction in Japan, mainly because of my physique, which they decided made me look like a miniature sumo wrestler. I wasn't crazy about that comparison (or about being called Kirby-San), but it was okay because I happen to like wrestling a whole lot. In fact, most of the Twins are wrestling fans, but especially Hrbek and me. If wrestling is on the TV in the clubhouse, most everyone will be glued to it. (I'll watch just about any sport, even ice skating. I found out during the Winter Olympics that I enjoyed that sport, too. The only thing I won't watch is golf. I refuse. I'm a terrible player and I won't watch. The whole subject makes me upset.)

I've seen guys miss infield practice, they were so enthralled watching a wrestling match. What TK had to say about that, I'm not sure. A lot of the WWF (World Wrestling Federation) wrestlers like Jesse "The Body" Ventura, the Road Warriors, Baron Von Raschke, Sergeant Slaughter, and some of the other guys live in Minneapolis and they stop by the Twins clubhouse every now and then. A standing invitation. Von Raschke is Hrbek's good buddy. The Road Warriors are mine. Don't laugh at these wrestlers. It's real! I promise.

I remember the first time the Road Warriors came by.

Hawk and Animal. They were massive. Hawk greeted me with a slap on the chest, like they do to one another. To them, it probably doesn't seem like they're hitting very hard. But when Hawk slapped me, my eyes started watering and I was doing everything I could to keep my cool. Al Newman said I had a very strange look on my face.

"Did you see what he did to me?!" I asked Al, gasping for breath.

"Yeah! Go get him!"

I just looked at the huge handprint on my chest and said no thanks.

Not long after that I was in a restaurant with Tonya when Hawk and Animal came in, and Hawk said, "Hey, buddy, how you doin'?" and—again!—he slammed me across the chest. Tonya jumped up and said, "Don't hit my husband like that!" Thank goodness she was there to defend me. These guys really don't know their own strength. The handprint on my chest was as red as an apple.

I had fun in Japan—we won the series—but if my career in America ended tomorrow and people said, "Well, you can come over to Japan and make a million dollars," I wouldn't do it. They don't have the facilities comparable to our major league facilities. They're way behind in that area. The clubhouse in Tokyo was the best clubhouse but the others were minimal. One of them only had one urinal and one commode for our whole team. I'm a short guy by American baseball standards, but I was tall over there. Even I had to bend over to get dressed in some of the clubhouses. Think about tall guys like Fred McGriff!

The stadiums are a lot smaller. We had sellouts every game, but that's only forty thousand people at the most. Some of the infields were all dirt. The pitchers' mounds are not raised nearly as much as ours in the States, which required quite an adjustment by our guys, who said they had to bend their backs all out of shape when they pitched. I don't pitch, but I still wouldn't go back to play ball in Japan full-time. However, look at what an opportunity it was for Cecil Fielder before he returned home to join the Tigers.

S E V E N

The Twins may not be flashy, but we're loose and loud in the clubhouse, and Puck can take part of the responsibility for that. That's me, Puck, the nickname everyone has finally settled on after trying out, over the years, a lot of others. Brunswick was one of the candidates. You know, the bowling ball. Not a bad name for me, actually. If things are quiet when Brunswick rolls into the clubhouse, he gets 'em stirred up. He's a main instigator. He'll make those pins fly! Other nicknames include Stub, Fire Hydrant, Fire Plug, Buddha, Pit Bull, Cannonball, Cannonball Head, Hockey Puck, Bucket Head, and some others that escape me at this time. My favorite . . . Puck.

Brian Harper and Puck can get the clubhouse festivities going on just about any subject under the sun. In the first place, Brian doesn't like my nickname for him, "Ravishing Rick Harper," after the wrestler, Ravishing Rick Rude. But the two look alike, I can't help it. Ravishing Rick Harper grew up out in the sunshine on the West Coast. I'll tell Harper that I hate California, he'll fire back that he hates Chicago. That dispute's always good for something. If the Lakers are playing the Bulls, watch out. The Pac-10 versus the Big Ten? I can hold my own in that one. Our prime time for this stuff is after we take infield, about half an hour before the game. Randy Bush says it's a good sign when Harper and I get into one of our loud "discussions" just before we head up the ramp for the national anthem.

Maybe I'll declare I'm gonna carry the whole team that night: "You just watch, hang on, we're going to win this game! I'll get the big hit!" Guys start jeering and we get excited and start yelling and having a good time and are ready to play. And if I do get a big hit, great. If I don't, or if I screw up, maybe I'll hear about it the next day. "*Please*, Puck, don't carry us tonight, okay?"

Against the White Sox in '92, somebody got on first base late in the game, a couple of hitters in front of me, and I spontaneously declared, "Well, boys, when I get up the game's over." Harper's batting fifth in the lineup, two behind me, and he tells Terry Crowley, our batting instructor, in a loud voice, "Well, I might as well not even put my batting gloves on." Lucky for me I hit a double and we won.

I'll go after Tom Kelly in the clubhouse. Did TK break my bat when he was throwing BP, or did he not?! Guys do not like to have their bats broken during batting practice, and TK and Stelly—bullpen coach Rick Stelmaszek—are good at that. But I always deny that TK broke my bat. And he'll say, "I snapped it like a toothpick!"

"No way, TK, no way! Don't be *lyin'* like that in front of your team!"

Kent Hrbek was one of the first guys to get on Tom Kelly *during* a game. Several years ago when the bats were slumbering, Herbie said, "Gee, TK, you don't seem to be doing too good. How about letting me manage this inning?"

Kelly called his bluff, "Okay, Herbie. It's all yours."

And Kent managed that inning. The bats are quiet, you challenge TK to wake them up, and he'll challenge *you* to do it. He's serious. Anytime you want this job, TK says, come and get it! A bunch of us have managed in the past few years. I managed for two innings in 1992. TK goes all the way down to the end of the bench and watches the action from there. If you need him to, he'll flash your play out to Ron Gardenhire coaching at third. Lots of fun, calling the hit-and-run and all that. I brought in a couple of runs in Chicago last year. I won an extra-inning game in the Metrodome against . . . I can't remember.

But Kelly can come back at me, or Hrbek, or anybody else, just as hard as we get on him. "Yeah, sure, Puck, that was a great at-bat last night! Really helped us out!" He doesn't have to specify which one he's talking about. I know, everyone knows, and of course it was a terrible at-bat and I'd be the first to say so, and probably did say so.

A few times reporters who don't know us have wandered into the clubhouse when TK and I have been going at it and they've thought, "Wow, man, the Twins exploded. The Twins have disintegrated." But, in fact, that kind of energy release is one reason the Twins *don't* disintegrate no matter how the season's going. Kelly knows that we have total respect for him, and the kidding around that looks like a lack of respect is just part of the whole Twins thing. Loosens everyone up.

No subjects are barred in the Twins clubhouse, either. In 1986, when I was the only black guy on the team and not long after Reggie Jackson had made an issue of this, the Twins were playing an exhibition game against the University of Minnesota Gophers. We called up a bunch of minor league players for the game, among them Danny Clay and Roy Lee Jackson—two black guys. I hadn't said much after Reggie's remarks, but now I walked into the clubhouse and shouted, "Lock it up, boys! There's three of us now!"

In 1983, the year before I joined the big club but was in the Twins organization in the minors, the Minneapolis Urban League charged that racial bias was the reason Ron Washington didn't get a chance at the starting shortstop's job in 1983. Of course the Twins organization dismissed the charge, and I had no way of knowing if it was true or not. But even Frank Viola's two-year-old son recognized in his own way that the Twins were thin on blacks on the major league team. This was some years back at one spring training camp, when six or seven black guys—minor leaguers—were playing with the team. One morning these guys happened to be more or less together in the clubhouse. I was off to the side or around the corner, but within hearing range. Frankie, Jr., walks in. You have to know that this boy had taken an instant liking to me, and I was one of the few, if not the only, black guys he saw much of. So what does he do but walk up to every one of those black ballplayers and say:

"Hi, Kirby Puckett . . .

"Hi, Kirby Puckett . . .

"Hi, Kirby Puckett . . .

"Hi, Kirby Puckett . . . "

They were totally confused, Frank was embarrassed, but I absolutely broke up.

Our clubhouse man, Jim Wiesner, isn't fazed by our antics on and off the field. "Mr. Baseball" just does his job. We've got the best-looking helmets in baseball because Jim polishes them every day. He even waxes down the catcher's gear. Our shoes are always immaculate. If you look at our cleats, they're A-one clean.

Have I changed much?

Batter up!

Getting to know the fans.

November 1,1986.

A moment with Mom
at my wedding.

Guess who makes his billboard debut.

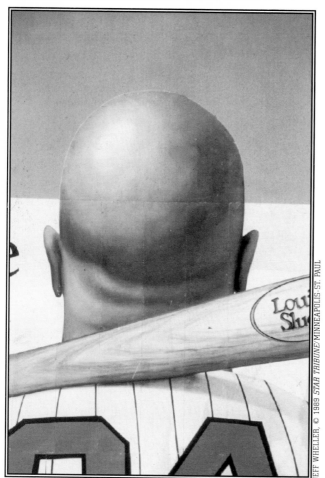

The Catch.

Celebrating our World Series victory in 1991 with my mother-in-law, a real Twins fan.

The Pucketts take the field.

Taking a breather between innings . . .

. . . and between games

Catherine Puckett, the real artist of the family

My new contract is announced—*now* Carl Pohlad and I can laugh!

The Second Annual Kirby Puckett 8-Ball Invitational. Left to right: Wayne Terwilliger, Carlton Fisk, Paul Molitor, Paul Gernie, Bo Jackson, Chuck Knoblauch, Eddie Murray, Dave Winfield, Yours Truly, and Cecil Fielder. Kneeling: Bob Costas and his son, Keith Michael Kirby Costas.

I love this game!

I've already said I like sharp shoes. The Twins have sharp shoes. Our uniforms never have holes in them. He takes good care of us. We even get little reminders from Jim before we go on road trips—useful facts and reminders about each city we're going to visit.

Jim more or less raised some of the guys on the Twins, going all the way back to minor league spring training camps. He probably started all the T-shirt giveaways that have taken the Twins by storm. Every year Jim produces a T-shirt for the team in spring training. In '91, the year we won our second championship, it read, "WORK HARD, PLAY HARD." Last year, "WORK HARDER, PLAY HARDER."

Everybody is always handing out T-shirts and other gifts and gags. When Hrbek hit his 250th dinger in Boston, he honored himself with a T-shirt. Chili Davis can always be counted on for a few during the season. His standard one is the "CHILI DOG" T-shirt. After the sixth game of the '91 Series, he produced one especially in my honor. On the front it read "PUCK" and on the back "JUMP ON. I'M DRIVIN' THIS BUS."

Do any other teams hand out gifts? I doubt it. I don't think many other clubs have so many family days, either. A few years ago guys started bringing their kids to the park on Sunday morning before those day games. Sometimes we didn't take batting practice that day, and the fathers had some time to goof around with their kids at the park. Everybody took part, whether they were single or had kids, and we had such a good time we turned one Sunday a month into the official family day at the Dome.

I think this team is also different in that everybody is sincerely interested in your well-being. How can we help you? Take Pedro "Petey" Munoz, a young Latin guy and the only Latin player with the Twins in 1992. When Petey joined us, guys went out of their way to help him get set up and make him feel a part of things. Shane Mack helped him get a car. Guys took him fishing. And nobody had to go around saying to the rest of the team, "Okay, now, we got this Latin guy. Don't let him sit in the corner." Including everybody and bringing them together is just the way the Twins do things. If it sounds obvious, check on some other major league clubs. I haven't played for them, but I talk and listen. Former Twins have gone to other teams and we discuss the differences.

With the Twins, if ten or twelve guys find themselves in the same restaurant for lunch at the same time, we'll drag together some tables and have a big banquet. It won't be four ballplayers here and four over there and four more in the back, like on a lot of teams. The Twins get the family table.

When I say, "I love this game!" I mean more than the action on the field. Getting close to a group of guys, playing as a team on and off the field, shooting the breeze and telling lies during our famous clubhouse tournaments of Casino, a card game I always seem to lose—that's what it's all about. When Magic Johnson retired he said what he'd miss the most was "the guys." I know just what he meant.

The Twins as a big family, the Twins "mystique" around the league: That's all true, and the feeling really took hold in 1987 and '88, but 1989 was something of a mess nevertheless, with a couple of uncomfortable situations in the clubhouse and our overall disappointing performance on the field.

That year got off to a bad start on Opening Day. Frank Viola won the Cy Young Award in 1988 after a brilliant season in which he was 24-7 and was basically unhittable with that circle-change of his. The previous year had been almost as good. Then the contract hassles started. Frank and his agent turned down $7.9 million for three years, Andy MacPhail said that he was through talking with Frankie's agent after the agent made Andy mad with some public comments, and then Frank ended up accepting the contract. By Opening Day the whole situation between him and the Twins and the Minnesota fans had soured, and he greeted everyone on Opening Day with an open letter announcing that he wouldn't be pitching for the team after that season. It was a shock. That was one of those times when there wasn't any joking about the situation in the Twins clubhouse. Then Frankie went on to lose that game and was booed when TK took him out in the seventh inning, bases loaded, nobody out. He lost his next four decisions, too, and the Twins lost eighty-two games altogether.

In July, as it became increasingly unlikely that we'd be in the pennant race, rumors of a Viola trade were a daily deal, although Andy MacPhail said he had turned down all offers. But he also said that the only two untouchables on the Twins were Hrbek and Puckett, leaving the door open regarding Frankie. One thing was certain, we needed pitching, and the Twins weren't going to trade an everyday player to get it. Viola expected to go in a deal for two or three pitchers, good prospects. I felt badly about the situation because people had turned against Frank, but we were good friends. Really good friends. Forget everything you may have heard about the problems in Minnesota that season. Frankie is a champ—one of my dinner buddies. One of our dinners in Seattle is now one of his favorite stories. The Twins arrived late at the hotel, and it didn't have twenty-four-hour room service, if you can believe that. (We have since changed hotels.) A bunch of us, including Viola, go down the street to this late-night restaurant. I'm just starving and ask the waiter to bring me something to eat, anything, whatever's fastest. Within minutes he brings me this plate and I recognize the chicken, but what's this other thing sitting there?

So I call the guy over and say, "The chicken's good but what's *that*?" Viola was probably already laughing.

"An artichoke."

"Artichoke! How many brothers you know eat artichokes?! I 'oughta choke' you for serving me this!"

I was just playing around with the guy—the tip proved it—and Viola, Mark Salas, a few other guys literally fell on the floor doubled up with laughter. I am not exaggerating.

In '89, we weren't laughing. Frankie started telling me in July that "it" could happen anytime, anytime. At the end of the month we were in New York and Frank told me in a restaurant that if he were traded, I'd be the first to know. One of the trading deadlines was coming up. That night—that very night—the phone rings in my room at two or three o'clock. A voice said, "It happened. It went down."

"Who is this? What are you talking about?"

"It's me. I got traded to the Mets."

"Come on, man. Don't kid me." Frank was a great kidder.

"No, I'm serious."

That was a serious trade, indeed: your Cy Young winner—the first time a Cy Young champ had been traded the following season—and an outfielder prospect for five pitchers—Rick Aguilera, David West, Kevin Tapani, Jack Savage, and Tim Drummond. West and Tapani were supposed to be solid major league prospects, and Aguilera was already a good major league pitcher for the Mets, so that trade was a roll of the dice for both teams.

Frank was strongly criticized for how he handled things

that year. A couple of the Twins even joined in, and that was unusual for our team, as I've explained. I did not join in. I never join that kind of stuff. I've said it before, I'll say it again: Everyone is different. We all do what we think is best at the time. For myself, I've never felt I wanted to be vocal in my contract negotiations, although I have expressed disappointment once or twice. Regarding that Viola trade, we missed Frankie, for sure, but life went on for the Twins. Frankie later presented everyone on the team with diamond watches in thanks for helping him in his World Series and Cy Young years.

A few weeks before the trade I had played in the All-Star game again, voted in by the fans for the second time, a big thrill, and I was then voted by the players and coaches in a *USA Today* poll as the best player in baseball. That just amazed me. Any player will tell you that being voted to the All-Star team by the fans is great, but extra recognition from other players is special because that has nothing to do with popularity and celebrity. That vote is just, "Can you play the game the way it's supposed to be played?"

I was even more excited about the trip to Anaheim when I found out that arrangements had been made for me to meet Willie Mays at Disneyland the Monday before the game. Just about my first question when I learned I was on the team had been whether Willie Mays would be there. He was one of my childhood idols and I'd always wanted to meet the great man. My all-time favorites were Ernie Banks and Billy Williams, Cubs players, because I heard all the great broadcasts by the Cubs' announcer Jack Brickhouse. But next on the list was definitely Willie Mays. He was the complete ballplayer. He could run, hit, catch, throw, steal a base; anything you wanted, he could do. I used to say to myself, I want to be like Willie Mays one of these days. I still want to be like Willie Mays, but I think I'll end up several home runs and RBIs short of his totals, 660 home runs and 1,903 RBIs.

In Anaheim I talked to Willie Mays on TV and told him how he used to be my idol. He said he had been reading about me and he appreciated my saying that I wanted to be like him. We shook hands and I gave him a hug and he hugged me and that was it. It was everything I expected.

Gary Gaetti was also on that 1989 All-Star team, and this was the season in which Gary's conversion to born-again Christianity became such a big story in Minnesota. "Rat," as we called him, was on that All-Star team for the good reason that he was a terrific third baseman, hitting and fielding, one of the best I've ever seen or played with. When I joined the Twins, he and Kent Hrbek were great models of enthusiasm. They played hard, screamed a lot, and had a great time playing the game. When I saw the way they played baseball, I knew that's how I wanted to play the game, too.

On the field Gary just had a certain fire about him that any major leaguer would be proud of. You had to be in awe of this guy. If the opposing pitcher hit one of our batters, he'd go nuts. He'd yell from the bench, "When I get up there I'm taking you deep, I'm taking you out of the whole stadium." And he'd go up there and hit a bomb.

The most memorable of all those occasions was in Oakland the previous year, 1988, our first West Coast trip following the World Series in '87. The pitcher didn't throw at some other Twin; he threw at Gaetti himself. Big mistake! We'd beaten the A's badly the previous year, and I don't think there's any doubt Tony La Russa wanted his team to send us an early message for '88, in case we thought repeating in the AL West would be easy. On Friday night, the first game of the series, the A's took a big lead early, then Gary hit a homer and an RBI single, and we finally took the lead in the ninth inning. Shades of '87. Twins dominance. So La Russa brought in Erik Plunk to face Gaetti. Plunk was a hard thrower with a reputation for wildness. But he wasn't so wild that the fastball at Gary's head was an accident. No way. The rest of us were yelling and screaming from the bench. Gary ate a lot of dirt avoiding that pitch, but he didn't charge the mound or anything. He just picked himself off the ground and a couple of pitches later smoked a rocket over the wall in left. Vintage Gary Gaetti. If you want to, you could call his tour of the bases that night "Cadillacking," but in that case the pitcher deserved it.

Later that season Gary was laid up while recuperating from knee surgery, and that's when he was born again. Gary's life changed immediately. No more swearing, drinking, cussing, smoking, yelling at the other team. He and Hrbek had been roommates for years, and now Gary got his own room.

At one point in what became a very public story in 1989, Gary was quoted in the papers as asking what was more important, being a good ballplayer or having his personal life in order. Well, that's a good question. If Gary became a better person, if he treated other people better, if he felt better about his own life, what's wrong with that? I just stayed away from the subject. I was brought up in the Catholic church. I still make the sign of the cross at the plate, a habit my mother insisted on in case I got hit in the head, but I'm nondenominational. I'm not a born-again Christian, but I try to live my life as a Christian and I go to church just like the next person.

I couldn't really share whatever Gary was feeling, so I just left it alone.

But there's no doubt that the situation was a subject of discussion for many of the Twins. Some of the guys felt Gary just was not a part of the team in the way he had been. I felt we all had to pull together. That's the point I tried to make in our pregame stretching routine—a ritual for the Twins, when we talk about anything and everything a little differently from the usual clubhouse banter or game conversations. We just had to pull together.

A year later, after the Twins' dismal 1990 season, Gary left for California as a "new look" free agent. The Angels offered him quite a bit more money, and I'm sure Gary thought it was time for a change of scenery. We all wished him the best of luck, but injuries have hampered Rat's career for the past couple of years.

By the end of 1989 the only excitement left for the Twins was my race for the batting title. The franchise hadn't had a league champion since Rod Carew won in 1978, batting .333. Guys were rooting for me. The odd thing was that I wasn't hitting the ball nearly as hard or as consistently as I had the previous year, but Wade Boggs wasn't having one of his best years, either, and going into the final few games he was about ten points behind me. However, he'd just ripped off a sixteen-for-thirty-nine streak, and he was closing the year at Fenway Park in Boston, where he always hits great, and I was on the road in Seattle where, for some reason, I don't hit that well. The Kingdome should be just another domed stadium with artificial turf, and therefore good for me, but it's not.

Wade had won four straight batting titles, five of the last

six, but this year I was in front and my destiny was in my own hands, where I like it. If I hit, I win. Simple as that. Carney Lansford was actually my nearest competitor. Carney had won the crown in 1981, the season shortened by the long strike. He was a career .290 hitter, and people thought that meant I should win, but they don't realize that the difference between .290 and .330 is not very much for short periods of time. It would all depend on who got hot and who got lucky.

Tonya joined me for the last weekend in Seattle. My mother was ill but I talked to her on the phone, of course. I was hitless—0-for-7—for the first two games, so my lead of four points going into the weekend was down to basically nothing by Sunday, the final game of the season. I was so nervous I decided my best strategy would be to go up swinging. Patience might have seemed like a better idea, but I was just too nervous. Fortunately I got a first pitch that I could handle in the first inning, and hit a double. Then I grounded out. They were flashing Carney's progress on the board, and he was going hitless. At that point I could have sat down and won the title. TK came up to me in the dugout and asked if I wanted to do that. "You know I'm not like that, TK," I said. Let me win or lose myself. I knew Carney was a class individual and if the situation had been reversed and Tony La Russa had asked him if he wanted to come out of the game, he wouldn't have done it, either. Guys have done that, I guess, but it's not my way. So I hit again and bounced a double off the right-center field wall and was celebrating when the ball left the bat. No way they'll catch that one! While I was standing on second base they flashed the announcement that I had won the batting crown, and the crowd gave me a standing ovation. That was great, coming in an out-of-town ballpark.

That month had been pretty draining, I'll admit. We

weren't doing that well as a team and I couldn't take any days off because if you don't play, your average can't go up, and I thought mine needed to go up. And I got struck on my wrist and that swelled up, but I had to play. I didn't change my style, either. No time for experimentation! Hack, hack, hack and let the good things happen.

One of the more important days in the life of any ballplayer playing today was the day the major leagues signed that $1 billion contract with CBS in the winter following the '88 season. I had already signed my salary for that season at $2 million, avoiding arbitration and reaching that salary faster than any other ballplayer.

All the ballclubs made sure that everyone knew that their payrolls had increased by some huge percentage in the last few years. With the Twins, the standard line was that Hrbek and Puckett would make more in 1990 than the entire team earned when Carl Pohlad bought the Twins in 1984. But I didn't worry about that because everyone also knew that the huge contract with CBS meant that each club would immediately earn about $14 million a year from that source alone. The smaller clubs like the Twins pointed out that their local TV contracts were a joke compared to those enjoyed by the New York and Los Angeles teams—$50 million or more annually for the Yankees and Mets, $4 million for the Twins.

Even though the Twins were considered one of the "small market" teams, predictions started coming out immediately after the 1989 season that I would become baseball's first $3 million player for the following year, 1990. That's when I would be eligible for free agency, but Andy MacPhail made it clear that he wanted to sign me to a multiyear contract after the '89 season, locking me up before I was eligible for free agency. That was fine with me if the price was right.

He and my man Ron Shapiro had tried to come up with such a contract after 1988, but couldn't reach terms and so settled on the one-year, $2 million deal, with $200,000 in incentives. Negotiations for the long-term deal continued throughout the '89 season. Obviously, winning the batting title on the last day didn't hurt my bargaining position over the winter. Throughout that period we never wanted to make the negotiations public or threaten to go to another club. That's not my style; that's not Ron's style. But I'll also admit that by August I felt that the Twins would have signed me for that multiyear contract if they were going to at all. They no longer had Viola's salary to worry about, and they had some money to spread around. Other clubs had taken care of some of their top players, and I felt that the Twins could do the same for me. After five one-year contracts, a multiyear pact wasn't too much to ask for, in my opinion.

The Twins had started out at $2.2 or $2.3 million for each of three years, and I might have taken $2.4 or $2.5. I was pretty pliable, but the Twins wouldn't budge. So negotiations dragged on until the fall, when everything had changed dramatically. I had won the batting title and other players had signed for large sums. The level of salaries had jumped up. What had looked outrageous in the spring now would have been considered a fire-sale bargain for the Twins. Howard Johnson signed with the Mets for $6.9 million for three years. Mike Scioscia signed for $5.7 for three years. Honestly, those players hadn't put up my numbers year after year. So when a reporter asked me if I would now sign for $7.3 for three years, I said bluntly, "The discount days are over."

Tom Kelly once summed up his thinking about me when

he said, "Puck wants to play baseball, he wants to make money, and he wants to win." That's right, all three of those, but he didn't get the order right. The money comes third. I'd be playing baseball just as hard as I do now if I was paid $30,000 a year. *If* that were the going wage. But it's not, and after all those one-year deals with the Twins I thought it was very fair that I earn the full market value of my abilities. Tell me what's wrong with that. That's why I told the press that the discount days were over. I'm sorry if that sounds greedy; to me it just sounds sensible. And if the Twins didn't have the money, they couldn't pay me, could they? I know some reporters and fans don't like to hear that last idea—players are always saying that nobody is putting a gun to management's head—but it's the simple truth.

What can I do about the money? I've worked my behind off since I was five years old to get to this position. All I've ever wanted and worked for was to be a good major league ballplayer. I never thought salaries would be where they are, but it happened. I put my body on the line every day, and now it's a good feeling to know that when I'm through playing, my children will be taken care of for the rest of their lives, and if they manage their money, their kids will be taken care of, too! When I want to do something for other people, I can. It's a good feeling. I'm not saying I'm here to save the world or anything like that—because when you say things like that people start calling!—but I'm living out my dream every day when I go out to the ballpark and put on my uniform and receive, well, substantial pay. I really am living a dream. It's unbelievable.

In the fall of '89 the Twins finally came up to the $3 million annual figure, $9 million for three years—the highest salary in the game. By not signing me the previous spring, when I would have taken $2.5 million, maybe less, they lost at least $1.5 million. But now, by the fall, $3 million didn't look like the highest number I could bargain for. I had a new decision to make: Take this money or wait and see what happened. Ron and I had a long talk over the phone, and we discussed that shortly after I signed for that figure the gate to $4 million or $5 million might open. "King for a Day"—that was the phrase we used. But I didn't care about that, really. By then I had set in my mind what I wanted and felt I deserved in the market—$3 million a year—and it was more than I had ever imagined I would have. I was thankful and told Ron, "Let's do it."

Someone had to break the $3 million barrier, and I didn't care if I was immediately passed by. Sure enough, within days Rickey Henderson signed a $12 million deal for four years— one more year than I got. Then other guys did even better, and the press came back to me wanting to know if I was resentful, but I told them that I had signed my contract and would stick by it without regrets. Besides, I had known I'd be passed by.

Soon enough Kent Hrbek, who was a free agent that year, was offered a deal by Boston at more than $3 million annually for four years, but Kent turned it down and got five years from Minnesota. Andy MacPhail was then nice enough to go back to Ron Shapiro and say he'd work out a fourth year for me, for the '93 season. He said he hadn't known Kent would sign for that kind of money for five years. As it turned out, Andy never did get back to Ron about adding that fourth year to the contract, a decision he probably regretted after 1992.

I'm a basketball fanatic and had a clause written into that contract allowing me to play recreational games. That fall was also the first season for the Minnesota Timberwolves, our

NBA team. I went to all those 'Wolves games that year, when they were playing in the Metrodome—season tickets, four on the floor, front and center, Jack Nicholson–style. The next season the 'Wolves moved into the Target Center, and well before that season I went to the president of the team to talk about where my tickets in the new arena would be, and he had a chart of the seating and we picked out my four. I wasn't looking for freebies. I was paying just like everyone else. I had paid for my tickets the first year. When the season was about to start I called up to get my tickets and to write my check. That's when I found out that I couldn't have the four seats we had agreed to. The president told me he had had to give them to a sponsor. I was upset because we had a deal. We had shaken hands on it. I didn't think I was treated fairly. I haven't been to a Timberwolves game since then.

Life away from the ball field has a way of putting these salary numbers in perspective, and it did so with me that fall of '89. My mother passed away on October 28. She had been in the hospital with heart trouble, but I thought she was about to get out. Tonya and I had just returned home to Minneapolis after visiting her in the hospital in Chicago when I got the call that she had taken a turn for the worse. So I turned right around and went out to the airport, but it was snowing in Chicago and my flight was delayed for hours. By the time I reached the hospital late that night, Mom had died. She was only sixty-five years old. That was the hardest day of my life. But at least when I had last seen her I was able to tell her that I loved her. Now when I speak to school groups, I tell them that they only have one mom and one dad, so be sure to love them and be sure they know it, because they may not always be with you.

Now not a day goes by that I don't think about both of my parents. I idolized Ernie Banks and Billy Williams as baseball players, but Mom and Dad were the best people in my life. They taught me to be responsible and to respect other people's opinions and ideas. That's not always easy to do.

My mother and sisters didn't really like baseball at first, but they came to love it. My mother had all kinds of clippings that people would send her, and many she would clip out herself. She came to some of my games when I joined the Twins, although toward the end she couldn't manage the stairs at the ballpark. But she listened on the radio all the time—but only until the sixth or seventh inning, if the game was close. Then she'd get too nervous.

My brothers and sisters say my mother spoiled me because I was the youngest. I guess she did. I was the only one who never worked during high school. All my brothers and sisters had jobs to help out, but my mom wanted me to concentrate on baseball. I wanted to work but she just wouldn't let me. She wanted me to focus on baseball. She would let me mow my sister June's yard to make a little spending money. I was also the only Puckett kid who got braces. But, in my defense, by the time I needed those braces I was the only child still at home and there was a little more money to go around. But, all in all, I'll admit that I was spoiled rotten. (Tonya was astonished when she realized that, even as an adult and a major leaguer, my mother came in to make my bed when we visited her in Chicago.)

I'd always dreamed of being able to buy Mom a house, but when I was able to do that, she wouldn't accept it. She wouldn't even accept a condo. She'd hardly let me do anything for her, because she just didn't feel like she needed anything. She did accept some jewelry occasionally, but the only way to leave her any money was to put it on the table out of her sight, and then run out of the apartment. And sometimes I sent money by Federal Express. She had to accept that.

Mom wanted to see me become a professional baseball player, and she got that dream. She wanted to see me play in the major leagues, and she got that dream. Then she wanted to see me on the All-Star team, and she got that dream. Then she wanted to see me get married, and she got that dream. Then she got to see me win the batting title. Even though she was only sixty-five when she died, I know she's not complaining, so I'm not either. I thank God she got everything she wanted.

E I G H T

Perhaps the best way to describe 1990 is to say that it just didn't happen that year for the Twins or for me, and leave it at that. But the problem was, I couldn't leave it at that at the time, because '90 was the first year of my big new contract. One of the reporters wrote in spring training, teasing, I guess, but serious, too, that now there couldn't be any more slumps for Puckett, any runners not driven in, any more 0-for-4s. At $3 million bucks for the season, all-out effort wasn't good enough anymore. I'm known as the guy who doesn't worry much, and that's about right. Now I was told I'd better start worrying.

Ballplayers don't go around expecting much sympathy, but it doesn't make us feel great to read that garbage, either. Sure, I felt pressure going into '90, and at the plate my average with men in scoring position that year was about .340, normal for me, I'd guess, and I drove in eighty on a team that wasn't scoring a lot of runs. Nevertheless, the ball just wasn't cracking off the bat like it normally did. Then again, I reminded myself that the difference between .300 and .330 is not very great, but my ability to get that extra hit every week was the reason I was earning three million instead of $500,000. And in 1990 I didn't get that hit consistently. My good friend and teammate Al Newman lost patience with me a couple of times when I'd complain that I just couldn't hit the ball.

"Man, I don't have any sympathy for you! .295 and you're complaining?!"

Al was hitting .240, which he considered a great year. I'm hitting .290-something and having a bad one. I wasn't looking for any sympathy, but he couldn't have given it to me if he wanted to. He would just start laughing every time I'd tell him that the hits weren't falling for me. He'd say, "Yes, they are falling in for you, big guy, but just not the way they used to!" From his point of view, we were a last-place team and that was affecting my numbers and everybody's numbers. If anybody does get hot when a team is going sour, pitchers just start pitching around that guy. Indeed, I got real hot for a while in late May and June and tore the cover off the ball. I was hitting .345 on June 8, right up there where I belonged. Then came the All-Star game at Wrigley Field, a homecoming for me of sorts and a proud day, but then the bottom fell out for the rest of the season. During one eighteen-game stretch in August, I had exactly one extra base hit.

As the year wore on the predictions started appearing: Puckett may not hit .300 for the first time in five years, and he won't even get close to two hundred hits, and his home run power is way down. Actually, my homers fell off in 1989, when I won the batting title. I had nine that year.

Our last games of the year were in the Metrodome against Seattle, and despite my lackluster year I still had a shot to get to .300 with a good series. In the bottom of the eighth inning of the final game of the year someone figured that a hit would get me to .300. I'm up against Dave Burba. Matt Sinatro was catching, and I worked the count to 3-and-2. Suddenly Sinatro announces from behind his mask, "Now what have we here?! A guy batting .299, 3-2 count, here it comes!" What he meant was—good luck. Get a hit and I'm at .300. I thought that was neat of Sinatro. I think the ump said something, too, like, "Come on, Puck." The ump might make a statement like that on the last day of the year with nothing but that batting mark riding on the pitch. During the "real" season, never.

I knew that Burba would throw it hard because that's his pitch, and I knew he didn't want to walk me. I hit a bullet to shortstop and Omar Vizquel dove for the ball and then threw me out. Unbelievable. But I wasn't angry. I hit the ball as hard as I could, and once I hit it, it's out of my control.

I ended up hitting .298, with fifty-seven walks, the most I've ever had—and too many, I guess! I was unhappy about the Twins' off year and my own off year, but I was also unhappy that everyone was making such a big deal of it. People knew that I'd been close to my mother, and they wondered whether her passing away affected me. It affected me a lot off the field, but Al Newman would confirm that the ballpark was where I got away from that loneliness. He doesn't think my sadness hurt me at all that year, and I agree. Maybe I could point to the lockout in spring training that cost us valuable time, time I always need and use. But who knows what happened? Besides, 1990 was not a bad year, by any means. I didn't hit .250, after all. I didn't disgrace myself. I had those eighty RBIs. But I didn't bat .300 and I had only twelve homers. The previous season I had nine, and this was after years with thirty-one, twenty-eight, and twenty-four home runs.

Why, why, why? The reporters wanted to know why my home run numbers were down, and I had to repeat for the thousandth time that I am *not* a home run hitter. If I get them, fine, but they're not necessary in order for me to produce. Fifteen to twenty-five home runs: That's about right for me. That's what I hope to get, but if I'm short on homers, I can take care of business in other areas: average and RBIs. I try to explain this, but they don't believe me.

A related subject: I read or heard somewhere that I'm "not known" for second-half power. This surprised me, so I looked it up. I have eighty home runs in April, May, and June combined, and sixty-two in July, August, September, and those few days in October. That doesn't seem like a huge difference to me. Then I checked on RBIs, the more important stat in my case: 389 for the first three months of the season, 396 for the last months. Case closed on the question of Puckett's productivity for the last half of the season.

And I'll tell you this, Andy MacPhail would have no part of sniping at Kirby Puckett, and I appreciated that. Neither would Carl Pohlad. After my year in 1990, some other GMs and owners around the league might have said something like, "We give the guy a big new contract and look what happens." Instead, Andy said that the fact that .298 is a "down" year for Puckett just shows how excellent a player our center fielder is. And then he went on to explain that in a down year for the team, it's hard to have an excellent year, especially on a team that really does think like a team. Not as many guys are on base, there aren't as many game-winning clutch situations, not as many times when the adrenaline really gets going.

We weren't winning, but the Twins never got mentally or emotionally down that year. Never. We were in last place or close to it at the All-Star break, and we ended up 74-88, last in the AL West, one game behind Kansas City. But we never *felt* like a last-place team. Never. We didn't show up at the park expecting to lose, which is what you get on truly "last-place" teams. And a lot of that you can credit to Tom Kelly. TK likes to say that tomorrow's a new day. Our clubhouse was never like a morgue. I know I was still laughing and joking and stirring up trouble. We just couldn't get going, that's all. We played hard—nobody can say otherwise—but it just didn't happen. Some of the commentators and fans blamed the Viola trade, because we were using the pitchers we got from the Mets in that deal. Andy just kept saying these guys are good major league prospects, good pitchers, and we have to grow along with them.

As I said, I was getting some bad press—well, not exactly bad, but *questioning*—for just about the first time. I didn't let it bother me and I didn't hide from the writers. I didn't—and don't—blow people off who want brief interviews, although sometimes I have made a good excuse about having to go hit or something, I'll try to catch you later. But if that guy or woman does come up to me to talk twenty minutes later, I'll stop and talk. You don't have to have an appointment. After every game I'm sitting there on my stool. No hiding in the training room or in the lunch room. Let's talk face-to-face!

Then the reporter might say, "You guys have lost nine in a row, how do you feel?"

Really. I have a reputation in Minnesota for coming out with clichés, and that's true, I suppose. But let's face it, the press can *ask* some clichés, too. Take that "How do you feel?" question. What am I supposed to say, "Great, man, just great"?

During the Olympics in '92, one of the Minneapolis writers in Barcelona said he missed the Puck's famous rapid-fire clichés, and he gave this exaggerated example: "I just have to do my job. That's enough for me to worry about, man. I can't be worrying about nothing else, man. I just go up there hacking. If the pitcher beats me, he's a better man that time. I tip my cap to him."

The thing is, those clichés are all true. Here are a few more, and I'll stand by all of them: "It's a *game*, man, and the Twins play as hard as we can, somebody wins, somebody loses, and we all go home for the night. Life goes on and we come back and give it our best the next night. If this whole season is a bad one, life will still go on and we'll do our best to turn it around next year."

After the '90 season, life did go on and the Twins did come back the following year. We won the World Championship, in fact.

I'm never going to be the kind of razor-sharp interview who can always be counted on for the dynamite quote, the great rip against another player. I don't do that stuff. I just follow my mother's advice: If you don't know what you're talking about, keep your mouth shut. And if I don't have something good to say about somebody, I'm probably not going to say anything at all. This isn't just caution when talking to the press, trying to stay out of trouble. This is the way I feel.

I probably received the best press of my life after I'd signed the league-leading $3 million-a-year contract, only to have it surpassed almost immediately by Rickey Henderson. When Rickey was passed by several players and started mouthing about it, I refused to. The writers came to me like crazy asking *me* why Rickey Henderson does that.

"How do I know?" I said. "Go ask him, not me."

Of course, they wanted me to say something negative. But I wouldn't do it. Rickey lives his life the way he wants to, and I do the same, and I don't judge him and I don't think he judges me. Ask Rickey why he thinks his contract is so unfair.

Same thing with Ryne Sandberg. Rhino's contract with the Cubs had a couple of years to run, but that spring, when all the salaries skyrocketed, he was suddenly way underpaid by the new standard, and he wanted the Cubs to meet a deadline on a new one. Don't ask me about his motives. Ask him.

I'm always surprised that celebrities and athletes worry about stuff that's written about them. Obviously, there's nothing they can do about it. Plus, it's really not that big a deal. I can't control what reporters write. They have their jobs, I have mine. During that '90 season a book came out announcing something called the "Total Average" earned by each major leaguer, and I was ranked down the list because I don't walk a lot. I just laughed.

One exception is when the various baseball magazines come out in January. I'm excited to see where they pick the Twins, curious to see how they analyze our strengths and weaknesses. I do get excited, I admit it, and it also hurts if they pick the Twins last or just about last, which has happened several times since I've been with the team, and I know we're not a last-place team. I'll think about that for a while. But then I remember I'm not playing for the writers, anyway. I'm playing for myself and my teammates and the fans.

I'll have a problem if you rip the Twins and then want to be our best friend. The only time I can remember really confronting a reporter who was trying that kind of switch was one year when we were going bad—it could have been '89 or '90, I don't remember—and this guy was really on our case. He talked about us so bad, I got fed up. I mean, the paper's delivered to my house every day and I read it. I read it every day. Finally I had to tell this guy how I felt. I went up to him before the game and told him if he thinks this game is so easy, why didn't *he* put on my uniform and go out there and play. I told him I knew he had a job to do, but part of that job was to be objective. But he was no longer being objective, he was getting personal. We're bad, say we're bad, but don't gloat about it, don't rub it in with a lot of clever stuff and then come and smile in our faces and pretend nothing's going on. No. That won't get it. And then, when we start playing good, be sure to say, "The Twins are sure playing good!"

Yeah, *right*.

Most of the Twins get along with the press. Our worst "offender" for a while was the boss himself, TK. He got into a locally famous argument with one reporter. A chair was thrown, it seems, and I don't guess our management was too happy about that. TK's attitude toward reporters was exactly the same as his attitude toward players. He expected them to know their jobs and to be prepared. He had no patience with dumb questions. He had no patience with any question that came off as an attack against a player. If he thought it was necessary to criticize a player publicly, he'd do it, but he wouldn't tolerate being baited into it by the press. Tom would rather work out with the players before the game than sit in the dugout talking to whatever national media happen to be in town. He's just not interested in that stuff. So Tom quickly got a reputation on the Twins and around the league as a players' manager who defended his players. He cared more about us than about good press. He didn't suck up to anybody. We loved it. But after the '90 season the Twins hired a consultant to work with Tom and some others in the organization on dealing with the press, dumb questions and all.

The thing is, most ballplayers (and managers) just want to play baseball and then be left alone about contracts, salaries, "How does it feel?" questions, and all the rest. That's the truth. But that's not the situation and we understand that, too.

Shane Mack came over to the Twins from San Diego in 1990. Here was a guy who was a UCLA superstar, had played on an Olympic team, and was the eleventh draft choice in the whole country in 1984. Everyone knew Shane had all kinds of ability, but he had just never really delivered on it with the Padres. Why was someone with Shane's ability playing in Triple-A after five years in pro ball? Elbow surgery was part of the problem, but here was a ballplayer waiting to shine in the right circumstances, and Andy MacPhail went out and got Shane in the winter draft for $50,000. Quite a bargain.

The word was that Shane couldn't hit right-handed pitching because he was platooned a lot with San Diego. But Shane believed he could hit right-handed pitching because he did it in the minors. From the first day he showed up in our camp Shane and I became buddies and we worked on his hitting, along with hitting instructor Tony Oliva, and then, in 1991, with Terry Crowley. In San Diego, Shane looked around for a right-handed hitter who knew what kind of hitter Shane was and could work with him, but he never found that guy. Tony Gwynn, the Padres' great hitter, bats left-handed.

Shane and I have a lot in common as hitters. We don't swing at a lot of strikes, we don't walk much, and we hit .300 (now he hits .300!). One of his first questions for me was how I handle the hard slider from the right-hander, and I told him about not being afraid to be jammed. From the very beginning when Shane was facing righties, I'd be yelling from the dugout, "Shoulder in! Keep your shoulder in!"

I wouldn't say that I took Shane under my wing, like some people said, but we are like brothers now. He can be quiet and withdrawn and sit by himself in a corner of the dugout—in what Al Newman and I used to call "the section." I don't let him do that. I'm loud and boisterous, so Shane and I make a good team. He can also be very frustrating, and I've told him so. I love the dog tracks and one night I reserved us a table at the track near our training camp in Fort Myers. But Shane doesn't show, he doesn't call. There's nothing personal about this kind of thing. Always, *always* late, if he shows up at all. But I accept Shane as he is—although sometimes I won't let him use my bats if I've been stood up the night before.

And I still yell at him. If there are men on base and Shane takes a bad swing, I'll yell at him. I have another little saying that I call out: "Throw it out there, Big Boy. Let it troll." Then the rest of the dugout joins in. We're like a chorus. TK chimes in to remind Shane to get a good pitch first. I must say, the north country has been good for Mack. He hit .326 in '90, the bad year for the Twins, then .310 in '91 and .315 in '92.

We call Mack "Big Boy" after Bob's Big Boy Restaurants. Shane Mack can eat! You name it, he'll eat it. I'm telling you! You would not believe what Shane Mack eats. A typical day of eating starts way before the sun rises, when he wakes up in the middle of the night, hungry, of course. Calls room service and orders breakfast or something, anything, food. Seven o'clock he wakes up again, he's hungry again, and he orders breakfast again. One o'clock, he and I go out to lunch, or maybe he'll join me for my favorite soaps ("The Young and the Restless," "All My Children," "One Life to Live," and "General Hospital") and then we'll play cards or watch a ball game, and of course he orders from room service. Only we're in my room, so it all gets billed to me! (As soon as Mack signed his new contract in '91 I told him we were playing cards in his room from now on, and he could eat on his own account.) We get to the ballpark between two and three o'clock and he sends one of the guys out to McDonald's for a couple of Big

Macs. After the game he chows down at the big spread in the clubhouse. Then we go back to the hotel and he either orders room service again or we go out for a big meal. How many times is that? One, two, three, four, five . . . about six meals a day, and Shane's not that big, six feet, 185 pounds, and no fat. By the end of the season, he weighs even less. He *loses* weight eating like this!

I've also named Shane "Filthy MacNasty." If you notice, he always has the dirtiest uniform on the team. We have two or three different uniforms, and most guys will change into a new one after BP. Not Shane. Sometimes in a game he'll slide and rip his uniform and his shorts will be showing. He still won't change uniforms. He has no explanation for this.

After the 1990 season, Tonya and I adopted Catherine Margaret. I can't imagine life without her now. We named her after our mothers. For four years we had tried to conceive a child, without luck. We saw an infertility specialist. We had a lot of alternatives. Any couple who has gone through all this will tell you it's tough emotionally. Before Catherine, Tonya could get very sad sometimes. It was difficult for her to share in the happiness of friends who were having kids, because our situation was unresolved. It weighed on me, too. Looking back, someone might conclude that *this* was the reason I hit .298. I don't know.

Tonya also became overinvolved with our eight-year-old niece Keilah, who lost her own father when he was twenty-five. Keilah spent a lot of time with us and even had her own room in our house. Finally Tonya's sister Alicia had to remind her that she wasn't Keilah's mother. Tonya didn't speak to her sister for a long time after that, she was so hurt, but her sister had been right. We knew it was important to have our own child.

We weren't very knowledgeable about how adoption worked; we just knew we loved children and wanted our own. In fact, we had talked about adopting some children even if we were able to conceive on our own. I was fortunate as a boy, because I grew up with my mom and dad in a neighborhood where lots of the kids didn't have both parents, and now Tonya and I were in the position to raise boys and girls who needed a mother and a father. After we adopted Catherine, I had a talk about all this one afternoon in the outfield before a ball game with Tim Burke, a reliever for several different teams over the years. Tim and his wife have adopted quite a few kids from countries all over the world, and when asked why, Tim says, "Because we have so much love to give."

Tonya and I were surprised to learn that some black organizations don't approve of adoption. They see it as another way to buy and sell human beings. We just don't agree, and we don't understand how these groups would take care of all the children of whatever race who don't have families. We did not *buy* Catherine. The fee you pay in an adoption proceeding pays for the work of the agency. How could that be free? Our agency has now set up a task force focused on black couples, trying to find ways to lower the cost of adopting (which varies anyway, according to each family's ability to pay). We believe a lot more black couples should consider adoption.

We chose our agency after working with my friend and agent Ron Shapiro and the United Way, for which we do some work, to find out all the alternatives in the Twin Cities area. Ron flew in to help with the paperwork, and we had our first meeting with the people at our agency in October. Boy or girl? No preference. The adopting parents can be as specific as they want to be, but that just makes it more difficult to find a baby. Tonya and I didn't care about any of that. There was also the question of the "open" adoption, in which the birth mother (and perhaps father) and the adopting parents know each other, and even exchange visits, sometimes for years after the adoption. Some of the birth mothers and adopting couples want this, but Tonya and I didn't, so we would be adopting the baby of a birth mother who didn't want openness either.

We moved into our new home and busied ourselves with all those chores. We thought we would have quite a wait for a child. There's a waiting period for the birth parents to terminate their birth rights, and adoptions can get complicated.

But less than a month later, at 9:15 one morning, the phone call came. I was asleep and Tonya was half-asleep (even in the off-season we keep a ballplayer's schedule, which means we get to bed around 2:00 A.M.).

Tonya woke me up to tell me and started to cry because she was excited and nervous. I was, too. The social worker wanted to come over to show us a picture before bringing the child. We didn't need to see a picture, but the agency likes to do this anyway, so she brought us the picture, which looked like the prettiest girl we'd ever seen, of course.

That was about 10:30 in the morning, and we had about five hours before she would return with Catherine, and we were unprepared. Totally unprepared. We didn't have any milk or diapers or anything because we didn't expect to get a child so quickly. We called Tonya's mother and she and Tonya's grandmother met us at our house in nothing flat. We all raced out to our local department store. But none of us had any idea of what to get. Pink clothes, we decided, because the baby was a girl. Pink everything, it turned out. That must have been some scene in the store. The four of us headed in different directions and grabbed whatever looked useful. We had quite a pile when we were finished. The next morning we read about this shopping spree in the gossip column of one of our local papers. Someone at the store had called in with the scoop that the Pucketts had rushed in to buy $500 worth of necessities for their new daughter. $500? Who was counting?

That was just a wonderful day for all of us. What a rush of emotions when our social worker walked through the front door with Catherine—but one, mainly: joy. A joy like I had never experienced. We all had tears in our eyes and were running around the house, so excited we could hardly stand it. Maybe we should have known that this day was coming soon, because just the previous weekend we had been visited by Mike Jones, my childhood friend from Chicago, and his wife, Michelle, and their baby son, Michael, Jr.—my godson. That was one of the first times Tonya was truly happy playing with someone else's baby. We said good-bye to the Joneses on Sunday. Monday afternoon Catherine came into our lives.

You can say anything you want about my .298 batting average in 1990, but one thing you shouldn't say to me is, "Isn't Catherine just like your own?" That question really offends Tonya and me. As Tonya says, Catherine is our precious jewel. How much more "our own" can Catherine be? People should know better than to ask something like that, but we've heard it anyway. We feel that Catherine was born to be our daughter.

It didn't take long for me to acquire even greater respect for my own mother, who raised the nine Puckett kids without any help at all, while Catherine can be quite a handful all by herself. I'd say she's beginning to take after her mother, who's a little on the dramatic side. There's a lot of the actress in Catherine. "Oh, Daddy, my finger hurts," and I'll kiss her finger. "Oh, Daddy, my hand hurts," and I'll kiss her hand. She knows how to pull my strings, that's for sure. Catherine is fearless—and in this she does *not* take after Tonya. For years after we got married, Tonya would not stay in our house by herself when I was on the road. Her mother or one of her sisters would come keep her company.

Catherine has two godmothers: Delores Henderson, associate superintendent with the Minneapolis schools and a longtime friend of Tonya's family, and Lin Terwilliger, wife of the Twins coach Wayne, Tonya's best friend. Tonya and Lin are always together at the Metrodome and out on the road when both happen to be traveling with the team.

One of Catherine's favorite foods seems to be McDonald's french fries, so that's our favorite trip for fast food (although in the off-season I lay off all fast food). Mostly we stay at home and play inside or out in the backyard or on the driveway, because there's not much peace and quiet out in public. People mean well, but it just gets overwhelming. So we stay home and I haul out Catherine's toys and we play with all of them, rain or snow or shine. Tonya tells me all these toys at one time can be confusing for a child, but I haven't noticed that. We even play basketball. Catherine can sort of dribble and I hold her up so she can shoot for two points. She hasn't made a basket yet, but her time is coming. In a year or two she'll be able to play ball in the Dome on Family Day on Sundays. Tonya takes her to quite a few games at the Metrodome and she watches maybe three innings, waves to me during my first at-bat, then goes to play with the other players' kids in the huge locker room used in the fall by the Minnesota Gophers football team. Each kid has her or his own locker, complete with a name tag. If Catherine's present, it must be a pretty wild scene down there. Those babysitters earn their pay.

I've always had a weakness for Christmas, and now Catherine gives me a great excuse to indulge. This fits right in with my in-laws. The Hudson family has always spent their every last penny on presents. I match them, penny for penny! I also buy a lot of gag gifts, and I get a few, too. Tonya says I pout when I can't open the presents before Christmas. It's just not true. However, I do insist that we start at 10:00 P.M. on Christmas Eve.

Christmas at the Puckett household in Chicago was always a big deal, too, and we always got what we asked Santa for. In my case, that was something to do with baseball, ten times out of ten—a new bat, a new glove. After I married Tonya and moved to Minnesota, I made sure to deliver Mom's Christmas present in person in Chicago. I didn't just want to mail it.

I vividly remember one year in Chicago when Christmas came in July, and it wasn't a baseball gift. I saw an ad in a newspaper for a bicycle on sale, and I clipped it out and gave it to Dad and asked if I could have that bike. That's the one I wanted. He bought it that afternoon and carried it home with him on the bus, already assembled.

I look at a lot of things differently now that I am a parent. I learned from my mom that if I don't know what's going on and I'm not directly involved, I should keep my mouth shut. I still believe that, because I've seen people get in real trouble butting into other people's business, but I now believe there are exceptions to the rule. Four years ago, Tonya and I were riding in a cab from the airport in the Twin Cities to our home, at that time in Brooklyn Park. We passed a car in which a man, the driver, was hitting a boy riding with him in the front seat, slapping him hard enough so that the boy's head hit the dashboard. Another boy sat in the backseat. Tonya started knocking on the window of the cab and shouting. She told our driver to get on his two-way radio and call the police. The cab driver wouldn't do anything and I was also unsure what to do. We finally lost touch with the other car, but not before taking down the license number. The minute we got home Tonya got on the phone to the police. Then she followed up day after day. The child abuse people tracked down the household and found this man and some indications that what we had seen was not a one-time episode. He became one of their cases.

"See?!" Tonya said to me. "We got involved and maybe saved those kids." She was right. That happened before I was a parent. Today, I wouldn't hesitate in the same circumstances, even though, in Minnesota, you have to provide your name when reporting child abuse, and there's a possibility the other people will learn your name. I'd still report that license number immediately. If I see something happening in a parking lot or in someone's yard, I'll be much more likely to intervene right on the spot.

As terrific as 1991 ended up—a World Series victory—
the season started out pretty strangely. Even now, I'm
still kind of lost about exactly what was going on
with the Twins' "right field experiment." It started
late in 1990, when the Twins were going nowhere as a team,
and I told Tom Kelly I thought I could play right field. We had
four good outfielders, Danny Gladden, Shane Mack, myself,
and the new man, Pedro Munoz, a good hitter and a better
fielder than he's given credit for. My idea was that I had
slowed down a step in the past six or seven years. (I turned
thirty during spring training in '91.) For pure speed and the
best natural tools, I thought Shane was now the best defensive player among our outfielders. All he needed was to know
the hitters, and time would take care of that for him. So I
thought that everyone might be best served if I moved to right
field, Mack to center, with Gladden staying in left field and
Munoz filling in.

I could play right field and I liked it over there. For one
thing, you don't do quite as much running. Playing center
field, if the ball's hit to the shortstop, I'm running behind
there. If the ball's hit to second base, I'm running there. If a

guy's stealing second, I've got to run in and back that up. Center fielders are always on the move. Plus the center fielder's throw to the plate has to clear the pitcher's mound, either in the air or on the first bounce. Fans don't realize this, but the mound is a hazard for the center fielder's throw home. From right or left field, you don't have any pitcher's mound. You just throw it in there. All in all, left and right are a little easier to play, I feel, and I thought we might be better off with Mack in center and me in right. I told TK late in '90 that if he agreed with me and wanted to give the plan a try, I'd be all for it.

Not long after that, one afternoon in Cleveland, I glanced at the lineup on the board and there I was batting third, of course, but with a "9" by my name—right field. I looked at the other positions and "7" and "8" were allotted.

"T, did you mess up here?"

"No, no. Right field."

Well, okay. I could have used a little warning but I did fine that day, and after that Tom experimented occasionally for the rest of the season. As a team we had nothing to lose. I played all three outfield positions that season, in fact, to say nothing of short, second, and third! We ran out of players in a couple of games, and TK pulled me into the infield in emergency situations, shifting me to the position least likely to require fielding the ball. Good strategy, but I didn't feel I was too risky. I had been an infielder for years, and I still sometimes take infield practice. I can handle grounders okay. As it turned out, a grounder would not have been the problem. In one game, I started off the inning at shortstop and after a single, TK shifted me to second and Al Newman to short. The next guy hit a bullet to Al, who turned a double play. I don't think I could have handled that one. Two outs now, and TK leaves me at second base. The next batter hits a short fly to right field. I go back, Shane Mack comes in and we almost collide, but I hear him calling for the ball at the last split second and get out of his way. All things considered, I think outfield is my real home.

In spring training 1991, I was playing a lot in right field. TK asked me how I felt about that, and I said, "Great." I meant it, too. I thought it was a good move. I worked so hard that spring—right, center, and left field, just in case—and I felt comfortable everywhere. I was getting the angles on the balls coming off the bat and off the fence.

Opening Day in Oakland. First we have to sit there and watch the A's collect their American League Championship rings. That was a first for me, watching the other team get the glory, but I didn't find it frustrating. The A's deserved it. Then the game started and I was stationed in right field. Disaster struck almost immediately. In the fourth inning, with runners on first and second, Dave Henderson lofts a fly into foul territory down the right field line, I run over, glove the ball—and drop it. The ball was catchable. I had to run a long way and I got there, but the ball hit the heel of my glove. I closed the glove too early. It was my fault totally. That would have been the third out of the inning. Embarrassing, to say the least, on Opening Day with me in a new position, more or less. Then it got worse because Henderson followed that foul ball with a three-run homer and we lost 7-2. My error more or less cost us that game. What's more, that was the first start as a Twin for Jack Morris, who had signed with us as a free agent after a great but, he felt, underappreciated year (and career) with the Tigers. "Fossil," as Rick Aguilera nicknamed Morris, is a great pressure pitcher, as he would prove in Game Seven of the Series in the fall. But he also had a reputation for being so intense on the mound that he'd get mad at his fielders if they botched a play behind him. He had been vocal in Detroit when he felt he had been burned by the Tigers' notoriously sloppy defense.

What would happen now that I'd screwed up in his very first game with the Twins? Nothing. I muttered about blowing that play when I came into the dugout, and Jack didn't say a word to me. (Another significant footnote to that Opening Day loss: Tom Kelly pinch-hit for Kent Hrbek in the eighth inning with the bases full and the Twins losing 7-1. Tony La Russa had brought in a left-hander to face Kent, who hadn't done anything against the A's starter Dave Stewart, a right-hander. TK's message was plain: We're a team. I'll do whatever I think is best for the team. TK would also bring in a pinch-hitter—Al Newman—for Kent in our home opener a week later.)

That Opening Day fumble turned out to be my only mistake in a couple of weeks of playing in right field. I was charging hard and coming up to throw. Those baserunners weren't getting from first to third very often. I thought I was doing all right, and Shane Mack in center was doing fine, too, I thought, although the other fielders did have to be careful with Shane in center. He had the final call on any ball and he enforced that right with a passion. Demanded his rights as the center fielder! He frightened Dan Gladden a couple of times, charging out of nowhere to call Danny off and make the catch. Reckless abandon! That was okay, but Shane was also off to his usual slow start at the plate.

One day TK comes up to me in the clubhouse and says, "Let me talk to you a minute, Puck."

"Yeah, T, what's up?"

"That's it for the experiment."

"Why?!"

"Just tell me where you want to play."

"Well, I'm having fun in right field. I've played center most of my life so I wouldn't say I *don't* want to play center—"

"Where do you *want* to play?"

"Well . . . center field."

"That's where you play, then."

TK was tired of toying around with the situation and wanted to get it settled, one way or the other. Maybe he also wanted to give Shane a break from playing center. But I'd still go to left or right field in a minute, right now. Somehow some people got the impression in 1991 that I didn't like right field, didn't want to play there. Not true! Given a clear choice, I said center. But right field was fine, too.

The next game I'm back in center field and the rest is history. The Twins again defied all the preseason predictions and won the Series for the second time in five years. We hit great that year, but any knowledgeable baseball person will tell you that another reason we won was our solid defense.

I've always taken a lot of pride in my defense. It's the part of the game—and my game, I think—that people don't appreciate or mention. I'm out there every pitch saying, "Hit it to me, hit it to me." I don't make many errors. Some people complain that I play too deep, but I get the job done. You can't satisfy everybody, anyway. Fans write in to the paper sometimes, but I can't worry about that. Some guys can play shallow because they can go back on the ball, but I have to play the way it's best for me. I'd be stupid to play shallow and let the ball keep going over my head. I've got pluses and minuses, I guess, but it's hard for me to believe that I'm a burden to the team out there, playing where I do, a little deep.

One thing I can't do is dive for the ball. That's one part of down-in-the-dirt baseball that I've never learned. I just don't know how! I used to be so fast I didn't have to dive. I caught everything on my feet. Now I'm developing something of a sliding dive, sort of like Jose Canseco's slide. I'm not ashamed! I'll break that out if I have to, but it took me thirty-one years to learn it.

Fielding is fun. Funny, goofy things happen out there that aren't easy to pick up from the stands. Other episodes are pretty obvious. Scott Erickson was pitching for us one day and was having a rough outing. A ball was hit to Shane Mack in the gap and I was hollering, "Second base! Two, two, two!" Shane grabbed the ball and drew his arm back to throw—and the ball rolled out of his hand. This has happened to every outfielder, but for some reason in that game I got tickled. I was backing Shane up but when I got to the ball, I was laughing so hard I couldn't do anything with it. That game was already a mess and that play the icing on the cake.

In another game a few years back, before he was traded, obviously, a ball was hit between Tom Brunansky and me. Bruno called for the ball but I called him off and chased it to the wall. As I bent over to pick it up I hit my head against one of those poles behind the "baggie," as we call it. Those poles are padded but they're still pretty hard. When I hit my head I was knocked back four or five feet, without the ball. I rushed back after it and hit my head again and bounced off! Oh, man! The Three Stooges! Bruno was doubled over with laughter. I finally got the ball back in without the runner getting the extra base, and Bruno and I exchanged glances and snickered about that the rest of the game.

Bruno was traded to the Cardinals in the deal that

brought us Tommy Herr. I was sad about that regardless of how the trade ended up, because he and I were such good friends; snowmobilers, as you know. Bruno eventually moved back to the American League with Boston, and when he returned to the Metrodome as a visiting player with the Red Sox, he once crushed a line drive to dead center field. I thought this was one of those perfectly placed balls for me— just beyond the fence, perfect for robbing the hitter of a homer. I wanted that ball! I got back there in time, I thought, but when I got ready to jump I was right up against the tarp. That was unfortunate, because that tarp can sometimes act like a catapult. It'll pick you up, somehow, and throw you down on the ground. That's what it did on that play and Bruno had his homer. I'm sure he saw me rolling around on the ground as he trotted around second base. I know he was laughing as he ran around the bases. He stopped laughing only long enough to hit another homer late in the game.

Do the fans know that the key to good fielding is positioning? I'm not sure, but I feel that positioning is one of my strongest points defensively. Name any hitter in the American League and I can tell you pretty much what he wants to do with the ball on any particular count. Anybody! I know what to do. I'll move accordingly in center field.

For example, Don Mattingly. At this point in his career Don uses the whole field, kind of like me, but if you come inside, he'll go for that porch down the line at Yankee Stadium. I play him straight up against right-hand pitchers. Against lefties, I shift him a little to left.

Rickey Henderson? Straight up. Then with two strikes, I'll make sure the right fielder cheats in a little bit because Rickey'll just try to poke his bat out to meet the ball. Rickey and I are pretty good friends, always playing around and joking around. He's a crazy guy to be around, and sometimes he gets a bad rap. I'll never forget one game against Oakland when Rickey and I challenged each other one-on-one. In the first of two episodes, he was on third base with one out. I had warned him before the game, "Hey, I know you like to run, but don't you run on me." He said, "Man, you know I gotta run."

Pop-up to fairly short center field. I charge the ball, catch it, and come up throwing as Rickey tags and races home. My one-hop strike to Brian Harper nails him. Out at the plate!

As I was running in and Rickey was running out between innings I called over to him, "Don't run on me, man! Don't do it!"

An inning later, I hit a ball down the left field line and I'm hauling for the double. Hauling hard! I'm going, going, going—when all of a sudden Rickey throws me out. I was just stunned. Now he comes running in and says as he passes, "Gotcha! Got ya back, didn't I!?"

There's a lot of that individual rivalry in baseball. It's most obvious between pitchers and hitters. The best pitchers want to get the best hitters out, and the hitters want to put the wood on Roger Clemens or Nolan Ryan. You look forward to the weaker pitchers because you know your odds of getting a hit are better, but you look forward to Clemens and Ryan and Guzman even more because they're the challenge, and that's what the game is all about.

A strange twist on this duel is when you're facing a guy who was a teammate for years. The competitive juices really kick in then. Frank Viola and I are best of friends in baseball, I love the man, but when he came back to the American League from the Mets and we faced him for the first time in Boston, I wanted some hits badly. Frankie and I had traded some serious barbs in our playing days with the Twins. I'd tell him it's a good thing he wasn't facing me with that circle-change of his—"You'd *better* keep that junk off the plate!"—and he'd come back, "Oh, it'll be off the plate, Puck, 'cause I know you'll swing at it out there!"

For the first time in our careers, we duked it out in Fenway Park.

First at-bat: 3-0 fastball, hard grounder, double play.

Second at-bat: hanging slider, slammed to center, Death Valley at Fenway, caught for the out. I glanced at Frankie trotting back to the dugout, he glanced at me. We both knew that ball was long gone back home in the Metrodome. Definitely.

Third at-bat: another double play on a slider.

Fourth at-bat: fastball up and in, tattooed to right for the single.

One-for-four. I can accept that against Frankie.

The experts were dead wrong picking the Twins to finish low in the standings in 1991, but they were right about the month of April. The Twins are bad in April, and you can look it up. In the eight months of April I've played for the Twins, we've had a winning record just twice, in '85 and '87. In 1991 we were 9-11. This is something of a puzzle, because I don't believe anybody prepares harder during spring training. But when the games start counting, we can't hit and we can't field in April. As a team, that is. I usually get off to a fast start, and did in '91. Maybe we're overprepared as a team. I don't know. But I still wouldn't change anything in the spring.

The experts were wrong about the rest of the season for two reasons: We had not been that bad a team in 1990, even though our record was lousy, and we had made a lot of improvements in the off-season. Take Jack Morris. He had almost come over to the Twins as a free agent in 1986, but his price tag at that time—$2 million—was too steep for us, according to the reports in the papers. In '91, the Twins met his price and our opponents paid the price. Jack's a winner, pure and simple. Take Chuck Knoblauch, our rookie at second base whom anyone could see after a few games was already an all-around threat, a gamer. Take Chili Davis. We had the stuff in '91! Nobody on that team was surprised when we won the Western Division.

I felt really good about the Chili Davis acquisition because Dan Gladden and I had helped convince him to come over to the Twins. We had a vested interest. Chili had always told me he wanted to play with me, and when he became a free agent, the Twins were interested. Gladden had played with Chili in the minors and then in San Francisco, and they'd been good buddies for a long time. Danny and I thought Chili could help our team, even though he'd been doubted because of his back problems and criticized for his outfield play. That situation is a standing joke, and Chili even takes part, but don't let him fool you. He can hold his own in the outfield. In any event, Chili is a perfect DH for the American League.

When we knew the Twins wanted Chili, Danny and I told TK we'd like to call him and try to convince him to come to the Twin Cities. I guess we did a good job. I don't know how often players get involved with "player acquisition." That was my first time, and I'm glad I did it. I don't think we'd have been in the Series without Chili's twenty-nine homers and ninety-three RBIs.

Among the players, Chili immediately became famous for his willful participation in what became known as the "Cajun Chicken Fettucine episode." (You may have noticed a number of food episodes in this book; good food commands a high priority in the lives of itinerant ballplayers.) Al Newman and I had a favorite restaurant in Seattle, a seafood place we'd visit every time we were in town. Terrific pasta and anything else you want. Al and I talked about this place for weeks before we got to town, so by the big day a large party of Twins was anxious to join us.

Shane Mack, Newman, and myself got there early (very unusual for Mack to be early). Shane ordered the Cajun Chicken Fettucine, which comes topped off by a large jalapeño pepper. Al and I had ordered the dish before and recommended it to Mack, but we always set the pepper to the side. We considered it decoration. Nobody of sound mind would eat that thing, we were sure, although I would sometimes take a little nibble.

We warned Shane about this jalapeño but he said, "These things aren't hot. These aren't anything compared to the ones where I come from." He grew up in Southern California. So he popped the entire pepper in his mouth and started chewing. His eyes exploded! He gulped his water, my water, Al's water, and then signaled for more water. He was still on fire. He drank some soda, ate some ice cream, nothing helped. We found out later he should have eaten some rice, but we didn't know. That may have been the first time in his life Shane Mack did not finish a meal!

Okay. Now Chili Davis and the rest of the guys finally show up. We tell them the story of the pepper—Shane still can't talk—and Chili says, "Man, I'm used to hot food, bring me a *bowl* of those peppers." Newman and I glance at each other. But then Chili eats the whole bowl. No problem. Doesn't even need water. Eats them like I eat oysters. Just amazing. They must have hot food in Jamaica, where Chili's from. Maybe his name is the tip-off.

• • •

Despite the homer in Game Six of the '91 Series that made me momentarily famous, despite my hot streak in the playoffs against Toronto, despite my .319 average for the season, that season was my toughest in baseball, as far as hitting goes, tougher even than 1990 when I didn't quite hit .300. I just never saw the ball real well in 1991. I had one hot streak in July—hot according to the numbers—but I never felt I carried the Twins, not for a single week. Your number-three hitter should do that every so often. Chili Davis carried the Twins a lot more than I did. Shane Mack was our best batter after the All-Star break.

I looked at videos with Terry Crowley a lot more than I ever had. I spent more time than I ever had down in "the hole"—the area down the right field line in the Metrodome that has a batting cage, where Terry works with anyone on various drills to get the bat through the zone quicker. I took extra BP, then extra extra BP. I worked on keeping my shoulder in, keeping my head still, timing my high leg kick. But I always felt a little out of sync. Kent Hrbek is always teasing me about his coming to the plate after I bat and hearing the catcher grumble about the pitch three feet outside that I just ripped to right for a single. "How did Puckett ever hit that pitch?!" the catcher wants to know. That kind of free swinging is great if I'm seeing the ball well. In 1991 I don't imagine Kent heard that complaint so much.

I worked on a lot of technical stuff that year, but I never tinkered with my basic philosophy—hit the ball hard somewhere if I get the chance—and I guess that pulled me through the year with decent numbers. But it also allowed me to lead the league in hitting into double plays (twenty-seven times), something I had never come close to doing before. Batters are always complaining that their bloopers that fall in for hits and the high choppers they beat out on Astroturf don't make up for their hard shots that are caught. In my case, I believe they do even out. I think they have to even out if you're going to hit .300. I know I get a fair number of high choppers every year. Al Newman calls those "Puck hits." Back in my first three seasons I got a lot of those hits, when I could really fly. Maybe in 1991 I wasn't getting them as often.

The season just proved that the Twins had really become a solid lineup in every respect. Of course everyone made a big deal about how we'd gone from last to first, but we knew better. Like I said, we never felt we were a last-place team in 1990. Every day in '91 it was another player making the key contribution. That's always the case with any world champion. It's always the case when you win fifteen in a row, like we did from June 1 to 16. That streak brought us from five and a half behind Oakland to a half-game ahead of them, and we never lost that lead. We were tied for first once or twice, but we never fell totally out of the lead. It's a lot of fun to win fifteen in a row. Hrbek handed out cheap sunglasses in honor of number twelve. That burst of victories, most of which were played at home, naturally, also got the crowds back in the Dome. Before that, it was lonely in there—fifteen thousand or so. After that we packed them in.

Can a season turn on one pitch in mid-August that was called a ball instead of a strike? I don't think any ballplayer believes that, but if it's possible, that pitch would have been Dennis Eckersley's delivery to Chili Davis in the ninth inning on August 16. It was a Friday night and the Metrodome was jammed for the first of a four-game showdown with the A's, who were trailing us by four games. (Chicago was closer, a game and half back.) The A's led 4-2 going into the ninth inning with "Eck" on the mound. This was not a promising moment for the Twins; we hadn't beaten him in fifteen tries since he became the closer for the A's. He was perfect against us, but we didn't feel badly about that because he was perfect against everybody else, too. But in this game, on a two-and-two count to Chili, leading off the inning, Eck's trademark slider off the outside edge of the plate was called a ball by John Shulock.

It doesn't happen! Eck stared in at Shulock. I don't know what catcher Jamie Quirk said, but I'm sure it was choice. On the next pitch Davis tripled, we rallied for two runs to tie the game, Quirk got tossed from the game in a later inning after going berserk over a play at third base, and we won in the twelfth when Chuck Knoblauch moved around the bases on a couple of little rollers by me and Hrbek. We won the next two games and that was that.

We had the division won by September, then beat the Blue Jays in five games in the playoffs—winning the last three in Toronto, to everyone's surprise. I was one-for-seven in the first two games and when the press asked me about that I replied, "Yeah, but we're one-for-two." I wasn't worried and I said so. I'd get my hits. Also, like any major leaguer, I'd take playoff and World Series victories over any individual honors. Those things are great, don't get me wrong, and I have a trophy wall in my basement that I'm real proud of, with all sorts of balls and bats marking this or that plateau or award. But if the team wins, that means a lot of guys have sacrificed themselves for the whole year. Everybody had to lay down the bunt or hit the ball behind the runner to the right side or hit the cutoff man instead of making the flashy throw all the way to the plate. I'm sure Wade Boggs would trade a bunch of his batting titles for just one World Series ring. In 1991 I already had one ring and I'd go hitless if it would help the Twins win a second one. But that would not help the Twins. Thank goodness I did finally catch fire in the last three games: eight-for-fourteen, two homers, six RBIs. Felt good, felt good! Mike Pagliarulo had our biggest hit, a tenth-inning pinch-hit homer to win Game Three. Typical of the playful Twins was Hrbek's line to Pags later in the clubhouse, when Pags was delayed by all the requests for interviews.

"You got one hit," Herbie says. "Big deal. You're holding up the bus."

We squashed 'em in Game Four, came back to win Game Five, and here we were again, the amazing Twins in the World Series for the second time in five years. We're not as glamorous and as hyped as the A's, but the record will show we're just as good.

Before the series against Atlanta started, Al Newman and I agreed that our previous victory in the World Series didn't make the job any easier in '91; in fact, we felt it might have made it a little harder. We felt even more pressure to win again because we knew how great it was, and we didn't want to feel the other side of the coin. We didn't want to get there again and not win it. We also figured we had the advantage because, like in 1987, we had four home games in the Metrodome. And even though we won all three games in Toronto's Skydome, let's not kid ourselves, the Twins win more often at home.

The reason is simple. We have that much confidence playing in our building. Tom Kelly preached to us from the first day he took over that this was *our* house and let's keep it our house. Don't let anybody come in here and mess up our house. These are our fans, so let's give them what they pay for. People are always asking me—off the record—if I truly like playing in the Dome with that baggie out in right field, all the noise, the dangerous roof—dangerous because you cannot take your eye off the ball as an outfielder. My answer is, on and off the record: I love the place! Like TK says, this is my baseball home, the only one I've known as a major leaguer. The Puckett apartment at 4444 South State Street on Chicago's south side wasn't the world's most glamorous, but it was our home, it was where I was loved and taken care of, so I thought it was a good place to live. I wouldn't argue that the Metrodome is the prettiest park in the league, but it's my baseball home and these are my fans, so I love the place. You bet I do. Also, it's better now than when I started with the Twins. For my first year or so, the baggie wasn't installed in right field. There was just a low fence out there, and pop-ups would go out. (Even then I didn't hit homers.) There was not much air conditioning, or it didn't work right. Anyway, it was hot. The lights were bad, although not for me, because they've always been worse for the right and left fielder.

People have called the '91 World Series the greatest in history, with five one-run games, three of those extra-inning games, four games decided in the very last at-bat, Game Seven an excruciating 1-0 in ten innings. Sounds great to me—but "greatest"? I don't know. I do know it was a helluva lot of fun to play, nerve-wracking, too, and a great pleasure to think about later.

Everybody knows the Twins won the first two games at home and proceeded to Atlanta with a big controversy brewing. Did Kent Hrbek push Ron Gant off first base before tagging him out in Game Two? I don't know because I didn't see the play. I could understand why the Braves were so angry but I couldn't understand the death threat against Herbie that was delivered to his mother. It's a game, man! But there it was, and before the Twins were introduced on the field in Atlanta for Game Three I asked Kent, "Now, you're not going to act the fool out there, are you?" After all, he'd be standing next to me on the foul line during the introductions because I was batting behind him in the lineup. An unfriendly greeting was guaranteed; if the Braves' fans started throwing stuff, I'd be in the line of fire.

"Take it easy, Herbie, please."

"Okay, okay."

But Kent gets out there and the boos are pouring out of the stands and, true to his natural style, Herbie eggs them on, waving his arms defiantly, asking for more. I was watching the stands carefully, I'll tell you, but nothing happened except fifty thousand boos, and the rest of the Twins were introduced and then we played the game.

I told Shane Mack before that game that I couldn't wait to see and hear what it was like on the field during the famous tomahawk chop and war chant. I'd seen and heard that business on TV, but I knew it would be something else, standing in the outfield. And it was. Just awesome, everybody chanting and chopping in unison. It was like being right in the middle of the world's largest and best sound system. After a while it lost its appeal, maybe because we were losing the games to the Braves, but at first it was incredible.

But it wasn't the chop or the chant that beat us in Atlanta. The Braves played good baseball and got great pitching and handed us three straight losses. When they erupted in Game Five for fourteen runs, folks thought the Twins were finished. We had to win the last two games.

Before Game Six back in our Dome, the clubhouse was

pretty quiet when I walked in. Too quiet, I thought. Hey, this is the World Series. It's a privilege to play in the World Series, not a chore. Ernie Banks, one of the greatest ballplayers in history, and Billy Williams, too, never even played in a World Series, much less won one, as a lot of these Twins had in 1987. Sure, our backs were to the wall, but so what? That wasn't such a bad place to be. We'd been there against the Cardinals in '87 and ended up popping the corks. We could do it again. This was one of those occasions when my normally loud and loose manner was exaggerated for a purpose. My team needed loosening up.

So I'm extra enthusiastic, ribbing guys, and then I suddenly announce, "Jump on board, boys! I'm going to carry us tonight. Don't even worry about it. Just back me up a little bit and I'll take us to Game Seven." I had made such boasts before just to loosen things up, but I hadn't had that great a Series so far. Everyone knew that. But what the heck. I had the feeling! I was going to carry 'em tonight. Sure enough, guys started talking and we went on the field ready to play.

The Catch. Well, it was like a lot of other catches I and every other good outfielder have made. You see the ball, you think, "Maybe! Maybe!", you hustle back to the wall in time, and then pure instinct takes over. In batting, see the ball and hit it. In fielding, see the ball and catch it. You don't think about those leaping grabs. It was the third inning, and Terry Pendleton was on first base, Ron Gant batting against Scott Erickson. Ron caught an inside pitch flush on the meat of the barrel. After playing more than five hundred ball games in center field in the Metrodome, I know almost instantly whether any ball is going to the warning track, the wall, barely over the wall, or way over the wall. My first reaction on Gant's drive was, "Uh-oh! That may be outta here." But then I realized as I was racing toward the wall in left-center that it wasn't going out. I said to myself, "I can catch this! I can catch this ball!" And I got there, found the wall, jumped, and grabbed the ball against the windowpane. They say Gant kicked the dirt in disgust but I didn't see that because I was wheeling to throw back to first. The odds were good that Pendleton was way off the bag there. Actually, he was all the way around second base, and my throw almost doubled him off.

Major madness in the stands for that play. The fans were a good deal quieter in the fifth inning as I dangled helplessly on the wall in center field watching Terry Pendleton's two-run homer sail over my outstretched arm to tie the game. Gladden scored on my sac fly in the fifth to put us ahead again but they scored in the seventh to tie it again. I stole a base in the eighth (number 12 for the year), but didn't score.

So we move to the eleventh and definitely the most famous homer I ever hit. That's old news. What's not so widely known is the good memory I had to set it all up. When Al Newman and I saw Charlie Leibrandt get up in the bullpen, we both immediately thought back to 1987, when the Twins were trying to clinch the division championship against the Kansas City Royals. Leibrandt had started the game in which we clinched the tie. Al had started off our big rally with a double and then the next three Twins hit home runs: Puckett to the blue seats in right-center, Gaetti to left field, and Herbie to right field. The fans were going berserk, as you can imagine.

"I can hit this guy!" I said to myself four years later, when Leibrandt started warming up in Game Six of the '91 Series. When Leibrandt trotted to the mound to start the inning Al said, "Puck, here comes your man."

I said, "Yeah, he is." You don't want to get overconfident,

but it never hurts your attitude to know that you've hit a guy before. Plus I've always hit left-handers well, as almost all good right-handed hitters do. I hit a little over .400 against left-handers in 1991, leading the league in that category. All things considered, I wasn't unhappy when Bobby Cox brought in Leibrandt to start the eleventh inning. Cox was second-guessed about this decision after the game, of course, but Charlie had pitched well in Game One.

I was leading off. As Chili Davis and I were swinging our bats in the on-deck circle waiting for all the ads to finish on television, Chili said, "Go ahead and get this over with," and I said something like, "That's my plan!" The question was how. I asked Chili, "What should I do here?" He said, "Just make this guy gets the ball up." He was always telling me that, and urging me to take a pitch for once, and I'd say, "Sure," and then go out swinging at whatever was thrown. I'd been going after those marginal pitches the whole Series, just like I'd done against St. Louis four years earlier. In '87 I was finally able to settle down and get some pitches to hit. Four years later I was able to do it again, in the eleventh inning of Game Six.

The crowd was loud before I even stepped into the box, but then they started screaming when I was announced. It was absolutely spine-tingling. And I took the first pitch for ball one, down and away! I stepped out of the box and grinned over at Chili. He started laughing. The next pitch was also down and away, but called a strike. Then Leibrandt threw a ball up under my chin. The count was 2-and-1. The batter's count! The next pitch was a change-up, too, but over the plate and up in the strike zone—and then out of the ballpark! If pictures are worth a thousand words, I can stop writing and refer you to the photograph on the back of this book. I've never been as excited on the baseball field!

I was almost hyperventilating during the celebration. To flame out like I'd done in the clubhouse before the game to get the guys going, and then to deliver that game winner in extra innings. I was just overwhelmed. Bedlam, man, bedlam on the field, but when I look back on the game, one of the more interesting things that happened following that homer was the silent exchange between me and Al Newman. One look said it all: Leibrandt, Kansas City, 1987, my pregame pronouncement four hours earlier. We're so close, we didn't have to say a word. We just hugged in joy.

In the interview room later TK told the press about my boast in the clubhouse that everyone could just climb aboard ol' Puck in Game Six. Then the reporters asked me if I'd really said that, and I said yes, but I had to admit that I'd also said it many times before and things hadn't worked out in some of those games! The reporters all laughed. Somebody asked me if I'd be able to sleep that night. I said I'd get my rest when I'm dead. (It turned out that I didn't start sleeping well again until December.) I also said that whatever happened in Game Seven, it was just an honor to have played in the 1991 World Series. (Lonnie Smith must have felt the same way because before the first pitch of Game Seven he extended his hand to greet our catcher Brian Harper. They had been teammates on the Cardinals briefly in 1985. That was classy of Lonnie, I thought, and so did the rest of the Twins. I'm sure the Braves thought so, too.)

After Game Six, Tom Kelly had a few quiet words for me sometime in that wild scene, to the effect that I'd done all I could to get us to Game Seven, but we hadn't won anything yet. We had to keep focused. I didn't know it, but TK was really working on keeping Chuck Knoblauch from getting too high. Apparently he was just bonkers with happiness after that sixth game. Understandably so, for a twenty-three-year-old rookie who'd had a great season and now was playing in one of the greatest World Series of all time. But Kelly was right, we had to play one more game.

Before Game Seven there wasn't much to say. TK just reminded us that we might never get in this position again, so we should just give it our all and enjoy ourselves, too.

After we won the game and the Series on the strength of Jack Morris' ten innings of shutout ball and Gene Larkin's pinch-hit with Danny Gladden on third base (Danny, by the way, had been jammed on the pitch he legged out for a double), Al Newman and I did our famous "splash," a rare and special celebration. The splash is a high-five where we'd fall backward after leaping and clapping hands. When we saw each other in the wild scene out on the field we didn't have to plan it. We spontaneously splashed.

Morris was voted the Series MVP and he deserved it. As TK nicknamed him in spring training, Jack was "The Horse" for us all season. He won the first and last games of the Series, and pitched well enough to win Game Four. His ERA for the Series was 1.17. Pretty good. Pressure pitching.

But, to repeat, the main memory, the main emotion, the main fact about the 1991 World Series: We won, man, we won. That's all I know.

After the Series I got yet another nickname: Minnesota Squats, because I was the host of the First Annual Kirby Puckett Eight-Ball Invitational Pool Tournament. This was about a week after Game Seven, while I was still having a hard time sleeping.

For years I'd been involved with the Make-A-Wish program, which a lot of ballplayers and other athletes and celebrities work with. A terminally ill child makes a wish and this foundation works to make it happen. If this boy or girl is a big baseball fan and wants a visit from Kirby Puckett, he or she gets it if at all possible. Tonya and I also have a program in which we buy a block of five hundred tickets for kids from community centers who normally wouldn't be able to afford the ball game. We also provide hot dogs and Cokes for the kids. There are a lot of minority kids in the group, and that's nice because there aren't many minorities in the crowds at the Metrodome. We'd like to see more.

Tonya and I also wanted to become involved with an organization where my visibility in Minnesota could raise some needed dollars. We decided we wanted the work to have something to do with children, and also with heart patients, because both my parents died of heart disease. Ron Shapiro helped us search out various groups and we chose the Children's Heart Fund, based in Minnesota. That organization has brought more than six hundred kids to the United States for heart surgery over the last twenty years, and it also works to improve cardiac care programs in hospitals overseas. The Fund needed money and a high-profile person to help them with fundraising. I began working with them back in 1990 and was joined by Mountain Dew Sport, for which I was a spokesman. That company donated $25 for every single or walk I got, $50 for every double, $100 for every triple, $250 for every home run, and $500 for every grand slam. A lot of players around the league have that kind of incentive program.

My pool tournament would also benefit the Children's Heart Fund. Coming immediately after the World Series, the timing for the first annual event couldn't have been better. A lot of ballplayers sponsor celebrity golf tournaments to raise funds for charity, but we decided to have a pool tournament instead because we wanted to do something different, and because I don't like to play golf. I have "played" in a few events, if you can call it that. They have a golf tournament along with the Pepsi All-Star softball game, and one year I gave in and signed up for golf. I shot about 200. At the banquet that night they presented me with a special award: a can of tennis balls. One year I played in Kent Hrbek's golf event, and another in Frank Viola's. Every year Frankie hounded me about coming, and I was happy to help out financially, but I really didn't want to go make a fool of myself on the course. But I finally agreed. I got up to the first tee, teed the ball, waggled the club like I knew what I was doing, and then turned to the crowd and asked, "Know how far I can hit this golf ball?" Then I picked up the ball and threw it down the fairway and said, "That's about how far I can hit a golf ball." And then I walked away and cruised the course for the rest of the day in my golf cart, dispensing good cheer along the way.

The Kirby Puckett Eight-Ball Invitational was going to be a lot more fun for me, because I'm pretty good with the cue. Credit for that event goes to Tonya, because without her there would be no tournament and no money for the Children's Heart Fund. Organizing the tournament is practically a full-time job for her. My name is up at the top, but I wouldn't pretend that I put this event together. That first year, 1991, she and a friend did it all in three months. The 1992 event was a lot bigger and took even more time.

I'm responsible for inviting the players and getting all the baseball memorabilia from the guys around the league that we auction off. And then I do odds and ends—anything and everything else she tells me to do. (Regarding baseball wives:

People assume they have it made, and it's true they shouldn't have to worry about money. But the job is not very glamorous, from what I've seen. Tonya runs our household. She handles various secretarial chores for me. She handles the finances. She cooks. Sometimes she feels like she's a single parent for much of the time. For seven months out of the year she's in charge of everything—the house, the family, everything—because I'm gone. And when I am in town, our activities outside the house have to be limited, unless we want constant disruptions.)

In 1991 my tournament raised almost $90,000, with a lot of support from different companies in Minnesota and beyond. Louisville Slugger, Rawlings, and Nike—I use their equipment—gave merchandise to be auctioned as prizes. Brunswick donated pool tables and Campbell Soup donated $10,000 to the event. Dayton's, a major department store in Minneapolis, donated $15,000.

Even though one of the worst blizzards in history struck Minnesota the weekend of the tournament, all of the invited players except Cecil Fielder were able to get into town. The pool players were Cal Ripken, Jr., Bobby Bonilla, Chuck Knoblauch, Eddie Murray, Harold Reynolds, Chili Davis, Joe Carter, and Wayne Terwilliger, our first base coach. A ballroom at the Hyatt Regency in Minneapolis was set up like a ballpark, complete with concession stands and novelty stands. Fifty people paid $500 to play against those baseball players. Fans watched from grandstand seats that cost $25. We set up big screens so everyone could see the crucial shots. Cal Ripken, Jr., won the tournament. I didn't play well at all, although I lost a couple of close games I could have won. Then came the dinner and auction, which was handled by none other than Tom Kelly.

A few weeks later the Twins flew to the White House for the reception and luncheon with the President. Frankly, I considered passing it up because the trip in 1987 had been disappointing, but Tonya pointed out how bad it looked when Michael Jordan didn't go after the Chicago Bulls won their championship, so I said okay, we'll go. I wish we hadn't. Next time, I won't, not unless they change things. It's all political.

We didn't even have lunch with President Bush. He disappeared after shaking our hands. The groups of little kids seemed like they were there for decoration. The kids didn't meet the President; they didn't meet us. The wives were separated from the players at one point and we never really got back together. They served hot dogs and potato chips and it was a struggle to get even that because of the crowd. One player couldn't find his wife until the bus was ready to leave. The whole thing felt like an opportunity for other people to get *their* pictures taken with the World Champions. Politics. I'm a Republican—sometimes—and a Democrat—sometimes—but the two White House ceremonies I've been to were poorly done. Now that I think about it, I will go back a third time, if I get the chance, just to see how these new Democrats do.

T E N

I know the idea is real popular, but I don't necessarily believe that one crushing loss in midseason can ruin the season for a baseball team. The problem with this theory is that every team suffers "crushing" losses throughout the season, but some team goes on to win the pennant. The winner's losses don't turn out to be so crushing after all. The whole idea is mainly one of those stories that reads great but doesn't make much sense to the guys who actually play the game.

Nevertheless, the game that the "experts" will point to as the crushing loss for the Minnesota Twins in 1992 was against the Oakland A's on July 29th. We'd been playing great baseball for a month or six weeks before the A's came into the Metrodome. We couldn't do anything wrong, really, and led Oakland by three games. Then they came from behind and won the first two games of the series and we needed a win in the third game. No doubt about that. And we led by two runs going into the ninth when Tom Kelly brings in Rick Aguilera to close out the victory. Rick doesn't have it that night and gives up a three-run homer to Eric Fox, a guy up from the minors we'd never heard of. Eckersley closes us out in the bottom of the inning.

A tough loss, certainly. TK closed the locker room for a few minutes after the game and said as much. No use denying it, he said. The kind of loss that takes a few days to get rid of. But we knew that we were still tied for the division lead. Two months of the season remained. This was a team that had won two World Series in the past five years. We were supposed to roll over and play dead because of one at-bat?! No way. Milwaukee did come into the Metrodome and beat us three out of four, but then we went to Chicago and beat the White Sox three straight. If you had wandered into the Twins' clubhouse before any of those games you wouldn't have seen or felt anything different from what it was like in May or June, when we were on top of the world.

The best explanation for 1992 is that our pitching was spotty throughout the year, our power hitting was way off the pace of 1991, we had lost Morris and Danny Gladden to free agency, and we just didn't win the ball games we needed to. It was one of those years when everything fell into place for the A's, despite a bunch of injuries and the usual number of controversies for them, especially the trade of Canseco. When they needed the hit or the pitch, they got it. We didn't. For a while we couldn't do anything wrong, then they couldn't do anything wrong.

My season mirrored the Twins'. I was smoking early on, red-hot, pounding the ball, leading the league in all sorts of categories. I was getting so much press I was forced to use an alias when we registered at hotels around the league. Too many unwanted phone calls. All the Twins were getting them, I guess, after the World Series, but it was just ridiculous with me. I quit answering my phone, or I asked the front desk to take messages. But when people couldn't get through to me, they'd demand to talk to the traveling secretary. A lot of people know he travels with us on the road, and they'd demand to talk to him if they couldn't reach Kirby Puckett. After a couple of trips around the country he came up to me during some early road trip and said, "Puck, we're going to have to do something about this alias."

"Whatdya mean? Why? It's working great. I can sleep all morning!"

"Well, I'm getting all your phone calls."

I laughed long and loud and said, "Maybe you'll have to get your own alias!"

That's the last I heard about it.

But I'm going to go ahead and give him an alias: John Doe. John is a great guy with a tough job, taking care of all these pampered big league ballplayers, and I do my best to make sure the younger guys on the team understand this, just in case they start to hassle John about a late airplane or bus or something like that. John divides ballplayers into two categories—high-maintenance and low-maintenance—and the Twins are mostly low-maintenance, but occasionally someone loses his cool and tries to take it out on John. After a tough loss it's no fun to wait around for transportation, but that can happen and somebody might get a little rowdy with John. Then I might step in, or pull the guy aside, and say, "What do you want John to do, magically make the bus appear?! You know it's supposed to be here. You know he double- and triple-checked. Something happened. Give him a break." Or I might ask, "Would you rather be back in Portland?" That's our Triple-A franchise.

Usually I'm on John's side, but no one is safe on the Twins, not even the guy who hands out the meal money and the room keys. Early last year in Baltimore he gave me an opportunity to slide the needle in. We were in a hotel that was surrounded by construction while they were redoing the water-front and building the new stadium downtown. The previous year, 1991, I had seen a mouse in my room. A mouse. When I phoned John with this news, he took it rather lightly, so I called the front desk and told them about the mouse, and got a new room. Maybe one reason I was sensitive to that mouse was a creepy experience when I was still a boy in Chicago. My parents had already moved out of the Robert Taylor Homes, so I was a young teenager, I guess. All the newspapers at that time were full of stories about the "super rats" that were infesting the city. One day I was over at my sister June's house, near my parents' house, and my brother-in-law Tommy and I were down in the basement doing some chores. He opened the lid of the toilet in the basement and there was one of the super rats—a huge hairy thing rising up out of the water. Tommy slammed down the lid and shouted for me to come to see this super rat right in his basement. He opened the lid again and started poking at the rat with a stick, but I thought this would just drive the thing crazy. So we slammed the lid down again and ran for some Drano and poured that on the rat and flushed the toilet. The rat started screaming like crazy. We flushed and flushed and finally the super rat got sucked up. Fifteen years later, I didn't want to sleep in any hotel room with a mouse running around.

Then this past year the Twins are at the same hotel and this time another player sees a mouse. Probably a different mouse. I happened to be standing alongside John in the lobby of the hotel when this guy tells him about the mouse, and John immediately blurts out, "That does it! We're getting out of here!"

I shout, "Oh, yeah! See?! A black guy tells you about Tom

and Jerry in the room, you don't do anything! But a white guy complains and we're gonna move!"

Ouch!

Behind the scenes all year in 1992, of course, and sometimes not behind the scenes, was my contract situation with the Twins. 1992 was the last year on my three-year deal. I could be a free agent after the season if I wanted to. In the spring I sat down with Ron Shapiro for our annual review of my finances and my contract status. Andy MacPhail wanted to sign me, but he had already made it clear to Ron that the Twins couldn't pay me absolute top dollar. Ron understood that, I understood that, and I made it clear to everyone that I had no particular interest in breaking the record and being the highest-paid player in baseball. I didn't even know who that was at the time, or what he made. There was no thought at all of open-market free agency, either. I wanted to sign with the Twins, they wanted to sign me. In one of Ron's first meetings with Andy, the Twins' general manager presented his book of Puckett statistics with my picture on the cover and the words "Baseball's Best." That's unusual, Ron told me. You could put it down as just good PR on MacPhail's part, but I didn't. I thought it indicated an attitude that the Twins wanted to sign me with a minimum of posturing and hassles.

The fans seemed to be on my side. As my hot hitting and the negotiations continued, fans were holding rallies. Signs were unfurled in stadiums all around the league. My favorite was in the upper deck in Kansas City: "RE-SIGN KIRBY OR WE'LL JUMP."

When I hit the first grand slam of my career, in the

Metrodome against Detroit, the reporters asked me the inevitable question about a contract drive. Reporters like to write about guys "turning it on" in August and September because they'll be free agents next season, or because they're on a contract drive, that kind of thing. Once, in fact, I said the same thing to a reporter. 1986, I believe it was. We were out of the race and I said, "Well, it's time for the money drive," or something like that. I regret saying it now because it wasn't true. The reporters want answers and you give them answers. But there's no such thing. Not in my career, at least. I already had a contract that was paying me very well.

Think about it. If a hitter can turn it on so easily, why not turn it on *all the time?* Why ever turn it off?! Why not be the greatest hitter in history?! I'd be hitting .500 if I could do that! So I don't buy that stuff. I've had great final weeks of the season, and I've had so-so final weeks.

My contract situation was the subject of a number of clubhouse barbs and comedy routines. There was no reason to pretend the negotiations weren't going on. Randy Bush asked one day before a packed clubhouse, "Puck, who you gonna keep on the team when you own the Twins? Can I still be on the team?"

"Yeah, Randy. You're one of my main men. My main pinch-hitter." And for some reason I just let loose and went around the clubhouse announcing who was going and who was staying when Puck acquired the club with his new contract.

"Harper, you're outta here. Outta here!

"TK, you're gone. Sorry."

"What about me, Daddy?" That was Chuck Knoblauch asking. Sometimes he called me Daddy because I helped show him the ropes when he was a rookie.

"Skippy?" That's one of our names for Knoblauch, because when he first came up he spent a lot of time sitting next to TK. "I don't know, Skippy. I'll have to think about it."

By the time I was through it was clear the new Twins under Kirby Puckett's ownership were going to have to acquire some more players—and a manager. We had a great time that afternoon. But we were playing so well early in the year, everything was fun.

Brian Harper and I talked a lot about politics. "Puck," he said one day, "here's my suggestion. Don't sign anything until after the election in November. If Clinton wins, you'd better go wherever they'll give you the most money because the tax rate will be sixty percent. If Bush wins you can afford to stay in Minnesota for a lot less money because the take-home pay will be about the same."

"For once we agree!" I shouted.

In early May, the Twins went into Baltimore for a two-game series and I sat down for lunch with Ron Shapiro and his associate Michael Maas. They were pretty close to a deal with Andy MacPhail, and they wanted my final approval. The newspapers got it right when they reported later that the deal paid me $27.5 million over five years. That leak, by the way, didn't come from the Puckett camp, so it must have come from someone in the Twins, maybe someone who didn't like what finally happened. Another part of the contract was not reported: a complicated equation paid me so much money for ticket sales over a certain number. The other leak that came out about this time was *not* correct. Ron never asked the Twins to open their books for him, and the Twins never did that. It wasn't even necessary. Ron knew and Andy verified the general financial status of the Twins.

Ron felt that this deal acknowledged the realities of the

Twins' situation, and I agreed. I was ready to sign. At that lunch somebody suggested I call Donald Fehr, head of the Players Association. We knew that our union looked on me as a possible record-breaker, one of the first guys to go through another barrier—maybe $6 or $7 million—just as I'd been the first through the $3 million barrier three years before. But this deal wouldn't set any records or break any barriers. I didn't care. I wanted to stay in Minnesota, which isn't the largest market or the richest franchise. That's what I told Don Fehr and he said, in effect, "Look, it's your life. Is this good for you and your family? You do what you think is right. I appreciate your calling me."

That night at the ball game, Ron and Michael were down in their choice box seats and saw Andy MacPhail sitting in a box up above them. Andy waved for them to join him and that's where they shook hands on the essentials of the deal, but Andy made it clear that he had to sit down with Carl Pohlad for final approval, and that this would take a few weeks because the owner was busy on other business matters.

I thought we had a deal. Andy thought we had a deal. Ron thought we had a deal. In fact, our phone calls over the next couple of weeks were mainly discussions about my second annual pool tournament.

But late in May Ron was sitting in his office in Baltimore when he learned that Mr. Pohlad didn't want to make the decision at that time. I was home when Ron called me, and I have to say that I was just about as disappointed and frustrated right then as I've ever been. I told Ron, "Look, we've done what we could. Let's stop now until the season's over."

I meant it. When Andy came back to Ron three or four weeks later and asked if I'd accept the same deal now if Carl Pohlad agreed to it, Ron told Andy he wouldn't even ask me to reconsider. He knows me. When I said that's it for the season, that was it for the season.

I was frustrated with Carl Pohlad's non-decision, but I was also speaking the truth when I was asked about the situation on ESPN and replied that Mr. Pohlad is a businessman and I'm a businessman, and he has to take care of his business and I have to take care of mine. That wasn't window dressing. I wish Carl had agreed to the deal, but if he didn't think I was worth that money to the Twins, that's his decision. $27.5 million is a lot of money.

One of the papers quoted Carl as saying that he thought he could get me for less money in the fall. No comment, because I don't know whether that was an accurate quote. Not long after he nixed that deal, Carl said he'd sell the club at the right price—$73 million. He paid about $38 million in 1985. You can see why the players are wary when the owners are always claiming to lose money.

On June 3, Andy MacPhail made it official that the Twins didn't have a deal with Puckett, and that talks would resume in the fall. The next night I hit my second grand slam and the fans turned to look for Carl Pohlad in his box. The hitting binge continued. By the middle of June I already had eighty-four hits, forty-nine RBIs, twelve homers. Was I angry and getting my revenge? No. I was just hot, that's all. If I'd gone into a slump people would have said it was because I was in a funk worrying about the contract.

Toward the end of the month I started cooling off, and we went into Oakland for four games that were billed, of course, as the first big series of the season. And the Twins downplayed that, of course. We were two games behind them in the standings, then three back when we lost the first game. Then we took the last three and roared into July feeling good.

I was voted AL Player of the Month for June for the second consecutive month. Only three players have won that award two months in a row. Don Mattingly won it in August and September of 1985, and Edgar Martinez also, in 1992.

By the All-Star break we were two up on the A's and people around the league were starting to say we looked like repeaters. At the All-Star game itself, I just looked foolish. President Bush was making the rounds in the clubhouse before the game, greeting the players just as I was changing from my practice uniform to my game uniform. The timing could not have been worse: He reached my locker just as I was frantically trying to get my pants on over my long underwear. I didn't make it and the guys were cracking up as I stood there trying to look dignified, holding up my pants, shaking hands with the President.

Going into that now-famous series against Oakland beginning July 27, we were three games in front. Oakland won the first game 9-1, the second game 12-10, and that third game 5-4. Three weeks later we were five games behind the A's and turning in some terrible performances. After one 8-7 loss against Seattle in the Kingdome that featured every kind of mistake, TK said, "We stunk." After another game he was quoted in *USA Today* as apologizing to the Twins fans for our performance the previous night against Juan Guzman of the Blue Jays. Shane Mack brought that to my attention. I was surprised. That was a little harsher than TK usually gets in public. Usually he'll say what a good game the other guy pitched. And Guzman did pitch a great game that night. It didn't matter. Our manager was mad.

As the team struggled, the reporters wanted to see broken

mirrors, slit wrists, maybe some blood on the clubhouse floor. They mocked TK's "even keel" theory, the idea that in a long season you take one game at a time. That's true, obviously, but the reporters wanted to see some agony from the Twins. For the most part, they didn't get it.

For my part, if the reporters are lurking around waiting for me to break something, they'll wait forever. I had one seven-game stretch when I struck out thirteen times. Just embarrassing. But I also knew someone would pay down the line. There's no timetable for slumps, either for me or for the team. If God would let us know when the bad times are coming, maybe we could prepare. But it doesn't work that way. Plus, let's remember that this team won two World Series within five years. In our division we were up against one of the best teams in baseball—the A's. You can't expect to win every year. You can't expect to repeat. You try your best to do so, but if it doesn't happen, it doesn't happen. I'm not going to let this game drive me crazy. That's why I can usually smile at the ballpark. Usually. I don't take the game home with me. Usually. I know Tonya likes this. When I leave the ballpark I'm going home to my family, and the reporters and the other players and the fans are going home to their families.

One of the few times I lost this perspective was after a truly terrible game against the Indians in late August, the last loss in a three-game sweep for them. In the eighth inning we had Randy Bush on third base as the go-ahead run with nobody out, but Hrbek, Chili Davis, and I all failed to get him home. After that game some of their fans were doing the sweep business with brooms as we headed into the dugout, losers once again. TK was seriously upset and I didn't feel like talking to the reporters either. Things got worse when the writers came in from the Indians clubhouse telling us that

Mike Hargrove, Cleveland's manager, said we didn't look like the same Twins, we didn't have the old fire in the belly. That was like throwing gasoline on TK's fire. I got upset, too. Mike's a good guy, but until he has a championship team, or one that at least finishes second, I don't think he has any right to say stuff like that. I really don't. I know I would never say anything like that. We had a bad series, period. Leave it at that.

Right about then Cal Ripken, Jr., signed with the Baltimore Orioles for $32.5 million for five years. Cal is also one of Ron's clients, but I didn't jump right on the phone to ask Ron how this might affect my situation. We talked a week or so later and I congratulated him on the Ripken deal. We didn't talk about my negotiation because there wasn't one at that time. But not long after that Andy MacPhail contacted Ron again and asked him if I'd *now* approve the deal Carl Pohlad had turned down earlier in the year. Ron told Andy he wouldn't even ask me. I'd said I wasn't talking about it anymore that year, and Ron knew I meant it.

As the Twins were fading in the AL West the owners fired Fay Vincent and talk immediately began about a lockout in spring training the following year. The players were told by our union chief Donald Fehr to save our money. No problem, because I already do that. All of us were talking about how the owners were determined this time to get rid of arbitration and free agency. Ron and I had a couple of long conversations on these developments.

Back to baseball: A writer in Minneapolis knocked the Twins for possible complacency. Most of our guys had already won two World Championships; maybe the fire had gone out of the belly on this Twins team. Even Tom Kelly wondered whether there might not be something to it. You can never be sure about that kind of thing, but I do know that I, for one, was mentally and physically drained after that series against the A's. I just sat by my locker thinking about what we could have done differently, but I couldn't think of anything. When the A's needed the key hit, they got it. When they needed the key strike, they got. For our part, we just didn't get it done in the same situations.

I don't say we were shell-shocked, but looking back, it's clear that we didn't really get back on track the rest of the season. We stumbled the rest of the way. Before that series with the A's, we were 60-38 on July 26, the best record in baseball. And we were playing beautifully. You can win games and not feel like you're playing so well. We were on top of it in just about every phase of the game. But then—crash. From that point on the season was a grind. We lost to everybody and we lost *bad*.

Despite everything, when we went out to Oakland to play three games in mid-September we were six behind them, so a sweep would have given us a shot, but we lost all three games by close scores, and that was that for the 1992 Minnesota Twins. We would end up in second place with ninety wins, an okay season by any measure, but considering that we were the defending champs, considering where we had been two months earlier . . . frustrating. If you want to say we lost the fire in our belly, go ahead, the press sure did, pounding us daily about how bad we were. But I would just say that's the way it goes sometimes.

For myself, I had cooled off a little at the plate after the torrid May and early June, and then in August I fell out of the league lead. I found myself in a race with Edgar Martinez, a young guy from Seattle who hits in the tradition of Wade Boggs, and, for a while, with Shane Mack, who was enjoying his usual hot second half. (Boggs wasn't in the race this year.) By the last two weeks of the season I was hitting .327 and Martinez was through for the year with .342. He had shoulder surgery—and he needed it, too. The guy couldn't throw at all. When my teammates heard about this development, they did some quick math and told me that all I needed was to hit about .500 for the last two weeks. Mack was hitting .322 and needed a .750 streak.

No problem. Well, one problem. The first pitcher we faced in that stretch was Nolan Ryan in Texas. But I did okay off The Express, singling in the first, walking, then striking out. I got two more hits against Texas' relievers and jumped a couple of points. However, I needed more than a couple of points and never got really close to Martinez. But .329 ain't bad.

One of the Minnesota writers suggested that the fans might as well come out for the last games of the '92 season because those would also be the last games Kirby Puckett would play in a Twins uniform. He figured I wouldn't take less than Cal Ripken got, and he figured Carl Pohlad wouldn't offer more than he already had. So long, Puck. Another guy wrote a really nasty piece for some small paper saying he was sick and tired of my good-guy image. This reporter was hoping I'd go to some other team so he could dig up all the dirt on me and print it. What the heck, but my teammates got mad about that piece because there was a lot of garbage in it about other players, too.

That last homestand against Kansas City and Chicago got pretty emotional. Tonya stayed home for the final games. She was too nervous sitting in the stands. The very last game I received a standing ovation at every at-bat. I was also looking for one more home run, which would have given me twenty for the year, and therefore a season batting at least .300 with at least twenty homers, one hundred RBIs, and one hundred runs scored. Nice round numbers, but I didn't get that homer.

Every night the reporters asked me, "How does it feel? How does it feel?" Well, it felt exciting and enjoyable. And after all, I was far from sure that these would be my last games for the Twins. I was hoping they would not be my last games. I wanted to play for Minnesota, and still hoped we could reach an agreement. The Chicago writers speculated that the White Sox would be a perfect place for me to play, close to my home in Minnesota, family there, up-and-coming team, great new stadium a mile from where I grew up. All true, but it wasn't long before White Sox officials said they would not be pursuing me in the free agent market. They said that, but I still felt they might make an offer when the time came.

We closed the season in Kansas City, just when George Brett was celebrating his 3,000th major league hit. They had a grand ceremony before one of the games, and all the Twins clapped for George, one of baseball's truly great hitters. Then he stepped up to the mike to make a little speech. Imagine my amazement when, in the middle of it, he waves into our dugout and says, "Kirby, one day this is going to be you, so take notes." I tipped my hat. I hadn't talked to him about my situation. This was just out of the blue. He went on to talk about how wonderful it is to spend your whole career with a single team. It doesn't happen often these days.

I was getting all sorts of attention in Kansas City, some of it unwanted. After one of those games Tonya and I were sitting on the team bus waiting to return to our hotel when this woman sneaks on and throws herself in my lap. She'd been drinking, that was obvious. I tried politely to ward her off and called for the bus driver to come get her, while Tonya urged me in no uncertain terms to get the lady off my lap. Quite a scene. Finally they got her off the bus, and she never did get the autograph she was after.

A couple of days later, the season was over and I was back home . . . waiting. I had filed for free agency and was waiting for November 9, when teams could officially make offers for my services. Waiting for November 14, the date of my pool tournament. Waiting for a new brother or sister for Catherine, because Tonya and I were in line for another adoption.

It was an anxious period, I'll acknowledge, and I don't have many of those. Any friend or family member who came around the Puckett household probably felt the vibrations, mainly because of my contract situation. I had had off-seasons when I wasn't yet signed, but I always knew I would be signed, and by whom—the Twins. This off-season was a totally new experience. Since Carl Pohlad had turned down the deal early in the year, I had decided to go ahead and file for free agency and see what happened. I was curious, frankly. I wanted to see what other teams thought of me. Then when Chicago, the Yankees, and the Blue Jays all said early in November that they wouldn't pursue me, I was nervous. Given recent history, a player starts thinking in terms of collusion. Sometimes I just went into my study by myself and closed the door and sat in the chair, looking out the window at the leafless trees. I'd never done that before. One afternoon Tonya and I were talking about something and she stopped me and said, "Do you realize you just answered me like I was a reporter instead of your wife?"

A fan might now ask whether I was nervous about my contract *during* the 1992 season. Could this have affected my performance? I know Cal Ripken, Jr., said that his status as an upcoming free agent did affect his season. All I can say is, if my contract situation affected my play, it must have been for the better because '92 was one of my best seasons in the majors.

I've always been pretty good at separating whatever was going on off the field from the game itself. That's one of my strengths, I think. In general, I tend to hold my emotions inside. I got that trait from my mother. She might have been hurting, but you weren't going to see it. I'm the same way. I may have been anxious during the season about my contract, but you weren't going to see it, and I wasn't going to let it affect my play. And I don't believe it did.

Besides, let's face it. I knew I was going to play *somewhere* in 1993, very possibly with the Twins, and at a pretty good salary. Like Ron Shapiro said years before, the worst-case scenario for major league baseball players is still a great case, and we know it.

About a month after the season was over I had some business in a downtown skyscraper, one with balconies all around. I was sitting in an office on the twelfth floor when I looked out the window and about twenty people were standing on the balcony, holding up a big sign that read, "KIRBY, PLEASE SIGN!" I laughed and waved. That was neat. I wanted to remind these fans that I had tried to sign months earlier. Don't blame me, folks.

Eddie Murray won my second annual pool tournament and everyone had a great time, and we raised $210,000 for the Children's Heart Fund. That was the good news in November. The so-so news was that I came in second to Dennis Eckersley in balloting for Most Valuable Player. That was disappointing mainly because I've always felt, and most everyday players agree, that the Cy Young is for the pitchers (Eck had already won their award) and the MVP is for the batters, so to speak. But, no tears from me. The bad news early in November was that I didn't get a single offer in the free agent market. But nobody else was getting any offers, either, so I wasn't nervous any longer. There wasn't anything to be nervous about! Nothing was happening. There wasn't going to be a bidding war for Kirby Puckett this winter, it appeared. But Ron Shapiro assured me that things were going slower this year than in previous years because teams were waiting until after November 17 when they'd learn whom they had lost in the draft for the two new National League teams, the Colorado Rockies and the Florida Marlins. In fact, that draft was probably one reason I and so many players—way over one hundred—were free agents this year. Free agents weren't eligible for the expansion draft. If the Twins had signed me during the summer, one of the protected spots on their roster would have been taken by me.

Ron and Andy MacPhail did have a few conversations the first couple of weeks in November, and almost immediately after the special draft Andy called Ron with a new proposal, which was actually a step backward for me. The amount of money—$27.5 million—was the same as in the contract our owner Carl Pohlad had turned down in the summer, but now the Twins wanted to defer some of that money. The real value of the new proposal, Ron figured, was more like $25 million. I knew that Carl felt strongly about trying to hold the line for the benefit of the other "small market" franchises—we had taken this into account when agreeing on the contract over the summer—but did he really believe I would accept less money now? Discouraging.

As negotiations continued to poke along, Ron felt that, for whatever combination of reasons, the Twins were not being responsive to the situation. Something had to give, he told

Tonya and me. He asked us to sit down and decide whether we would seriously entertain going elsewhere, even if we would prefer to stay in Minnesota. He and Michael Maas had decided that one reason the Kirby Puckett free agent market was slow was that the clubs didn't really think I would leave the Twins. Ron had had a few calls from general managers in both leagues, and he didn't want to get back to them unless I really was interested. Ballplayers have reputations. Agents have reputations. I've already said that one reason I signed with Ron was that he has the reputation of being a straight shooter. I knew he didn't want to jeopardize that by playing teams off, one against another, in the Kirby Derby, as one newspaper called this business. Time and energy and credibility were at stake, so Ron wanted me to decide once and for all and for real: Was I prepared to leave the Twins?

My answer was yes. I was prepared to leave the Twins. I didn't want to, but I would if the Twins were really asking me to sign for less than the agreement we had with Andy during the season. You can call that ego or pride if you want; I call it wanting respect. Ron flew out to Minneapolis and we thrashed it all out one more time, and came to the same conclusion: Let's get serious about free agency.

Within days, Boston and Philadelphia got serious, too. They were interested in me, I was interested in them, and both of those teams could handle a contract in the $35 million range. Ron had some serious talks with one other team, too, which requested anonymity. And other possibilities might come up, once people knew I really was available.

Two meetings were set up: Boston on Sunday, November 29, and Philadelphia the next day. In an attempt to protect both of those teams, Ron tried to get me in and out of town without the news leaking out. I didn't care, but Ron didn't want the media to get the story and the teams to feel they were being used to jack up the price, and then be embarrassed if I went somewhere else. As things turned out, Ron had to chide himself for ever believing that there are any secrets in the world of Boston sports. After all, he had worked in the press room at Fenway Park while going to Harvard Law. He knew Boston is nuts for sports.

But he did try. The plan was for Ron, Michael Maas, and the Pucketts to rendezvous at the Boston airport on Sunday afternoon and proceed to the Four Seasons Hotel, where Tonya and I were registered under the name Johns. A few key people at the hotel knew of the plan and were prepared to whisk me away in back elevators. Cloak-and-dagger stuff.

Ron and Michael were standing around waiting for the Northwest flight from Minneapolis when Ron noticed a TV cameraman up on a balcony near the gate. Already?! He decided to find out if the cameraman was after me. He walked up there and asked the guy innocently, "Gee, is the governor coming in?" The cameraman looked at a piece of paper and said, "No, some new player for the Red Sox. Kirby Pickett . . . no, Puckett. Kirby Puckett. That's the guy." So much for my secret visit. Ron went out to talk to the chauffeur provided by the Red Sox to see whether he could help keep me from being featured on the nightly news. It didn't work. The man got the shots. We did slip into the Four Seasons, but before long reporters were down in the lobby and the story of my arrival in town made the local news. The "Kirby Watch" in Boston got so out of hand that one TV guy got suckered by a prank a day or two later and reported that a press conference had been called to announce my signing with the Red Sox.

That Sunday night we had dinner in a private room at the

Four Seasons with Red Sox president John Harrington, general manager Lou Gorman, and Elaine Weddington Steward, assistant general manager and a black woman (not too many of them in baseball). They set out to sell me and Tonya on the team, the organization, the city. The exchange concerning Boston's reputation for racial trouble was pretty frank. The Marge Schott controversy was in the headlines, and her name came up in the discussion. I think I made it pretty clear I wanted nothing to do with any team owned by her or by anyone like her. Several players had told me during the season, long before I got really serious about free agency, that I shouldn't even consider Boston—a bad place for blacks, they said. But then I talked with Billy Hatcher, who plays for Boston, and he said, "Hey, it's no worse here than anywhere else." That's what Elaine Weddington Steward argued, too. She said the club had a commitment to hire more blacks in the front office, and to play a role in improving race relations in the city. Ron suggested after the dinner that one reason Boston might want me badly was just that. Maybe they felt that a Kirby Puckett could be a positive influence in the city of Boston.

After dinner, the Puckett contingent discussed the issues and played some cards. I was impressed with Boston. I believed their presentation was sincere. I had visions of tattooing the Green Monster with about fifty line-drive doubles, and slamming the occasional hanging curve into the net above the wall for a homer. That night is when it sank in for the first time that I was seriously talking about playing baseball for someone other than the Minnesota Twins, the only professional organization I'd ever known. I was actually thinking about switching families, in effect. I was excited and a little fearful at the same time.

Then came Philadelphia. The Puckett group took a flight out of Boston to Philadelphia early in the morning and arrived with no fanfare. Phillies president Bill Giles and GM Lee Thomas met us at the airport and we drove around town for an hour or so. Ron reminisced about his days at Haverford College, located in a suburb of Philadelphia, and we went to Bill Giles's house and met his wife, Nancy, who made us feel right at home. Coffee for everyone else, diet soda for me. Tonya was impressed by how much Mrs. Giles does in the community with the Phillies wives.

Then we proceeded to Veterans Stadium and looked at the facilities there—and word immediately leaked out, of course. Tonya and I had the same questions we had had in Boston: Where do the little kids play during the game? Where are the best schools in town? What do houses cost? What kind of community programs does the organization run? I felt I knew the Phillies baseball team pretty well, even though they're in the National League, but we talked about how a lot of their guys—Lenny Dykstra, John Kruk, Dave Hollins, Darren Daulton—are my kind of player: all-out from the first pitch.

Just as in Boston, the Pucketts and the Phillies talked about everything *except* money and contracts, and when we got in the team limo for the drive to the airport, Tonya and Ron and Michael and I looked at each other and had the same thought: Philadelphia is interesting, too!

On that ride everyone agreed to give everything a couple of days to sink in, and Ron, in the meantime, would get back with Andy about the Twins' position. But there was no doubt that on Monday evening, the odds that I would re-sign with Minnesota dropped from 80 percent, say, just to draw a number from the hat, to 50 percent, to draw a lower number from the hat. The idea of change had taken hold, especially for

Tonya. And the prospect became apparent in Minnesota, too, with suggestions in the media that Puckett could be gone *fast*, and without the Twins really having a chance to match any other offer. They got that right. Ron had made it clear to everyone that the Twins would not necessarily be given the opportunity to match any other offer, because we felt that was unfair to those other teams. And it wasn't really necessary, anyway. Everyone knew the figures: the $30 million range for the Twins, $35 million or so, maybe more, for the teams in bigger markets. If I were offered $35 million by Boston, say, no one believed that the Twins would match it. They would not have. I'm pretty certain of that.

Tonya and I talked all day on Tuesday, back home in Minnesota. My good friend Frank Viola called me to lobby for Boston. So did Roger Clemens and Mike Easler, the new hitting instructor for the Red Sox. Jim Fregosi and Curt Schilling called me from the Phillies. All kinds of people called. I had talked almost daily, it seemed, with Chuck Knoblauch and Shane Mack and Chili Davis and other guys, and now we talked some more. I talked but I didn't sleep. Neither did Tonya. Only little Catherine was sleeping. And headaches! The Tylenol people owe Tonya and me big-time. I'd fall asleep at three o'clock and wake up at six o'clock, thinking about everything. One morning I was watching TV at six o'clock—that's how bad it got—and fell asleep immediately, then woke up several hours later to "Bewitched."

Lou Gorman for the Red Sox and Bill Giles and Lee Thomas for the Phillies called Ron frequently after our visits to those two cities, and Ron explained that he didn't even want to talk hard numbers until I was truly prepared to make the move. This wasn't saying that Minnesota had dibs on me, just that this decision came first in my mind. The other teams understood this. Ron put the number $28.5 million on the table for the Twins, and Andy started to work toward that number, but slowly.

On Wednesday, as the Twins still hadn't come to the 28.5 figure and Tonya and I were pretty close to deciding that we'd be living somewhere else next season, Ron read our mood and called Andy MacPhail and said bluntly, "Andy, this is going to get away from you, and one reason is we don't really know where you stand. We need action *now*." Andy immediately suggested we all get together. He wanted a dinner with the Pohlads, and soon he called Ron back with the official invitation for Thursday night. Ron called Tonya and me. It wasn't very convenient for him to fly in, but he was willing to. We were reluctant. My attitude by then was pretty simple: A fair contract offer—very fair, considering the market—was on the table. What's to discuss over dinner? It wasn't like in Boston or Philadelphia. I knew the Twins organization. They knew me. Did they want to sign me? That's all it came down to. Tonya and I were just really in turmoil and the idea of a dinner party was too much, but Ron suggested we give it a second thought. Stay calm, everyone. Maybe we owed Minnesota equal time, since we'd given two other teams the opportunity to make their pitch. Andy called me and urged that we come to the dinner, but I told him I thought we should discuss everything through Ron. I mean, that's why I hired Ron.

In the end, we decided we should go to dinner with the Pohlads. If they were kind enough to invite us to their house, we should be polite enough to go. We knew them socially through the parties Carl gives every year for the players and clubhouse and front office people who work for the Twins, but we had not been to their house.

Just before Ron got on the plane in Baltimore he received another phone call from Lou Gorman in Boston, wanting to get into high gear. The media in Boston were getting excited by the idea of a right-handed line-drive hitter taking dead aim at the Green Monster night after night. Lou Gorman said he thought we were looking for $33 million, and Ron said, "Lou, we're not going anywhere for less than $35." But Ron emphasized when he relayed this to me that this was a general *discussion*, not a negotiation, because I hadn't decided to go to Boston.

It was snowing Thursday night in Minneapolis when Tonya and I picked up Ron and Michael Maas at the airport and drove to the Pohlads' house. There I was, going to dinner with the owner of the ballclub that I had just about decided I wouldn't be playing for next season. I thought we were gone, really. If they hadn't come to a deal by now, what was going to change? It was strange that night, and I guess everyone was a little nervous, but we soon settled down, mainly because Carl and his wife, Eloise, were so friendly and gracious. We talked about Minnesota, the Twins, the state of baseball, family values, you name it. Regarding baseball, everyone was pretty honest in agreeing that the game is in a critical state. A lot is going on—labor wars included—that has nothing to do with the game on the field, and the fans don't like it. They're sick of it. Everyone in baseball knows this. We read the papers, we read the letters to the editor, we listen to the talk shows. But what can be done about it—that's another question, and we didn't come up with the answers on Thursday night.

Carl said he wished he'd signed me when he had the chance in May. (He said this again later at the press conference announcing my new contract.) He said it was his fault and he apologized. I don't really remember what I said to that. It was awkward. After visiting in the Pohlads' living room we went in to dinner, and all of a sudden Tonya spoke up about the subject of change. She was really emotional, and her deep feelings had an impact. She explained that she had spent her whole life, basically, in Minnesota. Twenty-seven years. She'd never really been away from her family. She'd never really felt her own independence. Going to Boston and Philadelphia had provided her with the opportunity even to *think* about change. The trip to the East Coast made her realize that a new town might be valuable for both her and me; it might be a good challenge. And we might have a little more privacy! I might be able to take our children to the playground. Tonya wasn't negative about Minnesota, not at all, she loved the state and would always call it home, but maybe a change for five years would be good. (So much for the quote in the newspaper from the anonymous ballplayer who said during the season that the Pucketts would stay in Minnesota because Tonya would never leave.)

I think everyone at the table was surprised at how openly she had expressed herself. I wasn't. I know my wife! If she has something on her mind, she says it. I also think Andy and Carl and Eloise understood that the Pucketts had given a lot of thought to the prospect of changing ballclubs. It wouldn't be something we did lightly, nor would it be something we were afraid of.

Right then, I wouldn't have been surprised if Andy and the Pohlads had thought, "Good Lord. Puckett's gone."

At some point Carl suggested a meeting the following morning, but Ron kind of shirked that off because he wasn't sure what I wanted to do now. As we left the house, Andy told Ron to call him *anytime* to pick up the negotiations. Both Carl and Eloise said again that they wanted us in Minnesota, but everyone must have wondered whether the hugs and kisses exchanged at the door were not really saying . . . good-bye.

On the drive to our house, and then sitting around the family room, Ron and Michael and Tonya and I talked about all the issues one more time. The situation was overwhelming for all of us. Tonya cried some. Now she was really concerned that people would say I left Minnesota because of the money, which wouldn't have been right. She was afraid that she liked the idea of moving more than I did. After all, I was the one who had played ball for the Twins for nine years; she certainly didn't want to force me into changing teams. She knew how unusual it is for a player to stay with one team his whole career, and that all the shifting of teams and players is one of the problems with baseball right now.

Ron reminded us that we couldn't make decisions based on what other people might wrongly think or believe. He also reminded Tonya that we wouldn't have much privacy in Boston or Philadelphia, either, not after I arrived in town as perhaps the highest-priced player on either of those teams. And don't let this become personal, he said. Just do what we thought best for the Puckett family.

Now Tonya was seeing a lot of good reasons to *stay* in Minnesota, and I agreed with all of them. I can't exaggerate how confused and up-and-down we were. The Pucketts were a basket case late Thursday night and early Friday morning.

What did I want to do? That's what it came down to, because Tonya said she couldn't be happy if I wasn't happy. At two o'clock on Friday morning, of all times, it was time for me to decide. I was tired of all this. It had been an exciting week and a lot of fun, but a lot of tension, too. I don't recall ever saying straight out, "I want to stay here," but I think Ron understood that was my decision. Tonya, too. I looked in her eyes and said, "Even if I could go out there and get as much as Barry Bonds, I guarantee you no one will have more happiness five years from now than we'll have here."

Ron asked, "What's fair for you to stay here?"

"Thirty."

For five years. That was understood. I thought the figure was fair, but I still had my doubts as to whether the Twins would accept it. In fact, I was the only one of the four of us—Ron, Michael, Tonya, and myself—who thought the Twins might still say no. But I also felt that if they did turn us down, I could leave the Twins with a clear conscience, regardless of what the fans might say.

Ron said, "Guys, there's only one way to do this. I'll call Andy now, give him the number, no playing around, and let's get an answer tomorrow."

Andy was sound asleep at 3:30 but woke up fast, Ron says. Ron gave him the figure and said, "Andy, it's yea or nay. Nothing in between."

"I'll call you back."

Later in the morning Andy called back from Mr. Pohlad's office, wanting to modify the interest rate on some money that had been deferred in order to help the Twins with their "small market" payroll problems. Carl is a banker, after all. Well, that just opened everything up again, as Ron had warned Andy it would. Ron and Tonya and I started discussing all over again the wisdom of change. But finally Ron just countered with some changes in the All-Star bonus, and he and Andy settled the business about the interest rate. The Twins agreed to Tonya's request to donate one thousand seats to each of thirty games each season of my contract, bringing kids to the Metrodome. Tonya will administer this program with the Twins. After a last series of rapid phone calls, the deal between Kirby Puckett and the Minnesota Twins was done by noon.

The emotion from the dinner the previous night carried over to the press conference at 3:00 P.M. There were several relieved baseball people and one relieved baseball player sitting in front of those microphones. I said that now I'll celebrate Christmas on December 4. Something that nobody really wanted to happen—my leaving the Twins—had almost happened anyway, for a whole bunch of reasons. But we saved ourselves in the nick of time. Maybe fans say, "Aw, come on! What's so hard? You want to play for the Twins, you come up with a fair price and sign the contract." But it's not that easy. The numbers are huge. They're hard to deal with. Plus the idea of change became powerful for Tonya and me. Most people can understand that.

As it turned out, what did change in my life after signing the new $30 million contract? Well, one big thing: Kirby Jr. Catherine now has a baby brother, and Tonya and I have a son. They're both worth more than $30 million to us.

Besides that, little changed except that my phone was ringing off the hook for days. Everyone seemed to feel I made the right decision! Were Tonya and I going to run out and build a fifty-room mansion or buy a million-dollar sports car? Not likely. We never even had a real celebration. On Saturday, the day after the press conference, I flew to Chicago to attend the benefit for two of umpire John Hirschbeck's children, who needed ultraexpensive bone marrow transplants.

Tonya and I did decide to buy a house in Fort Myers, Florida, where we can get away some in the off-season. That will be a change, and it will also be convenient because we can use the house during spring training. This does not mean, however, that I'll spend those days lying on the beach. A nice park with green grass and a swing set for Catherine and Kirby Jr. is a more likely outing; at night, maybe the dog track.

But in the spring of 1993, who knows? Four days after I signed with the Twins, the baseball owners voted to reopen negotiations on the labor agreement with the players, one year early. Talk of a lockout resumed immediately. I wasn't worried. I thought we'd play ball in 1993. Besides, I was too relieved to worry. Out of a million emotions I felt in the days right after the signing, the main one was . . . relief. It was over with. Never again! One day I had believed I was gone from the Twins, the following day I was back.

Our manager had been right from day one. TK said all summer, "No way Kirby leaves the Twins." I wish I had been so sure. In my heart, I didn't want to leave Minnesota, I didn't want to change teams, but only now was the question definitely settled. The day after I signed the new contract the Twins ran full-page ads in the local papers proclaiming that "THE PUCK STOPS HERE." That's right.

I'm a Minnesota Twin forever.